The Tuskegee Univer
continued relationsh
generations.

'*a*
all

.ndler

Archivist, Tuskegee University

In Critical Grace, *Cecil reminds us that what God was doing in Tuskegee, Alabama with Booker T. Washington and his cohorts was monumental. It was overlooked at the time, but the seeds of the kingdom of God were being planted, and those seeds inevitably sprout and bring forth the fruit of that kingdom. . . . We can see that right in the heart of Dixie, God planted a seed in the heart of a man that has consistently given light to darkness and pushed back the onslaught of hell's intention to divide and devalue His creation.*

Dudley Hall
President, Kerygma Ventures
Author of *Grace Works* and *Incense and Thunder*

I became part of the faculty of Tuskegee University to immerse myself in the culture to find the real "Spirit of Tuskegee" and the truth. Cecil's book has clarified that truth further, and I am grateful for his willingness to share. Cecil's story gave me much more "food for thought." The work Cecil has put into the content is evident and offers new perspectives on Booker T's overall purpose and message.

Edith Powell
Author of *More Than Peanuts*
Co-author of *To Raise Up the Man Farthest Down*

CRITICAL GRACE

INSIGHT BEYOND COLOR: BOOKER T. WASHINGTON'S VISION FOR LASTING RACIAL HARMONY

CECIL CARDER

ISBN-13: 978-1-95756-621-4

Cover Design by Tom Avery Graphics, Inc.
Interior Design by Niddy Griddy Design, Inc.

LCCN: 2024906140

Printed in the United States of America
1 2 3 4 5 6 7 8 9 10 Printing/Year 28 27 26 25 24

To Dianne

Contents

Foreword

Anything that I attempted to do for the members of my own race would be of no real value to them unless it was of equal value to the members of the white race by whom they were surrounded.
—Booker T. Washington

There is no greater story of tragedy to triumph than that of Booker T. Washington. He was a man born into slavery, who upon becoming free had only one desire—to get an education. Washington did not levy grievances due to his early childhood as a slave. No, he set his sights upon an education first and became one of the greatest orators and educators this nation has ever known. His commitment to getting an education, serving, and enabling others led to his purpose in life of building the first school of advanced education for Blacks in the South, Tuskegee Normal and Industrial Institute. It was there that his three-point strategic plan took hold: education, entrepreneurship, and self-reliance—truly conservative principles. For Washington, it was not just about the learning of books, it was about an industrial education that taught skills to advance his race "up from slavery."

Here is a man for whom we can credit such achievements as being the first Black man to speak on an all-white platform at the Atlanta Cotton States Exposition and to host a sitting US president at his institute, to visit the White House as a guest, to earn an honorary degree from Harvard University. Not to mention, we can credit Washington with recruiting one George Washington Carver, who became the father of agricultural research at the university level. Along with his school Tuskegee being the home of the first Black combat fighter pilots, the Tuskegee Airmen, of whom my godfather, William "Stickey" Jackson, was a member, Booker T. Washington was also one of the founding members of the Negro Business League.

However, with all these impeccable accomplishments, achievements, and impacts, this man who rose from the lowest of lows to the highest of highs has never received appropriate fame and accolades.

Why?

Because Booker T. Washington was a man of grace and profound wisdom. The opportunities he created were borne out of his belief that life begins at the bottom as well as his heart for making the world a better place for people of all races. He never allowed grievances to limit his belief in the goodness of humanity. His model of individual responsibility was rejected and replaced by an agenda to create and maintain a hold of economic enslavement within the Black community.

Washington's principles, ideology, and theories on life and character are needed today and more relevant than ever. These are just some of the reasons Booker T. Washington is my ideological mentor and role model. But Washington's story is not just for those with a darker complexion; it is for all of us. Grace not only transcends time, it also transcends race.

I was introduced to Cecil Carder in July 2023. After reading my books and hearing a speech I gave where I credited much of my beliefs to Washington, he determined that I would be a good candidate to write the Foreword for the book you hold. I believe in what he has written, and I was pleased when given the opportunity to introduce Cecil to those who may not know him. As you will read, his life has been changed by the Man from Tuskegee.

In his book *Critical Grace*, Cecil shares his experiences of learning about Washington and relates how Washington's writings have fundamentally changed his life and the way he sees others. Cecil talks about how we need to become more gracious toward each other, like Booker T. Washington. I love his idea of referring to ourselves as "Tuskegee Americans" and embracing the template of Tuskegee and what Booker T. Washington called the "Tuskegee spirit." If there were ever a time to reintroduce America to the character, wisdom, and grace of this brilliant man, whose story has remained hidden from even his own people, it is now. If there were ever a time to reemphasize the importance of education, entrepreneurship, and self-reliance, it is now. If there were ever a time to stress the importance of faith, spirituality, and character, it is indeed now. Now is the time for grace, and it's critical. Cecil not only retells the remarkable story of Booker T. Washington but does so in his own uniquely gracious storytelling style.

It is my hope and dream that we can restore Booker T. Washington to the place of honor that he should hold in America. Through this book, may many begin to see the Man from Tuskegee as an ideological mentor and role model, and may it help break the chains of race hustling as a means to make a living and gain power by those who make it their business to focus on grievances and perpetuating a slave mentality, overlooking possibilities and opportunities.

In 1961 when I was born in a Black-only hospital, there was a beach protest in Fort Lauderdale, a "wade in." Blacks could not go to Palm Beach Island in 1961, unless perhaps you were house servants. However, fifty years later in 2011, I was sworn in as the second Black Republican member of Congress from Florida and represented Fort Lauderdale Beach and the highest per-capita income zip code in America at the time, Palm Beach Island.

If Booker T. Washington could rise "up from slavery," then I could certainly rise up! His ascension is indeed a "harvest of glory." And after reading this book, well, in the old Southern vernacular, ain't none y'all got an excuse.

Steadfast and Loyal,
Lieutenant Colonel Allen B. West (US Army, Retired)
Member, 112th US Congress
Former Chairman, Republican Party of Texas

Preface

The thought never occurred to me to write a book about the relationship between the Black race and the White race. But God, who is rich in mercy, had something up His sleeve and led me on a journey that revealed His thoughts regarding the truth of why His children on planet Earth are so divided by the color of the skin He created.

In the fall of 2020, God began to open my eyes and reveal that we have forgotten there was a time, in our nation's history, when Blacks and Whites were growing closer rather than apart. While what divides us is ultimately the outcome of sin, not hearing the old stories of God's redemptive love and grace from our ancestors of both races has denied us the idea that we are better together. As I read the true stories of our historical past and glimpsed how so much moral high ground of racial harmony was being gained in the early twentieth century, I was made aware that our lack of retelling these stories has been a major contributor to the polarized relationship between the races.

Early one morning, God revealed what He had up His sleeve all along. It began to make sense as I was reading the last chapter of Booker T. Washington's autobiography, *Up from Slavery*, for the second time. It was in that moment that I heard the words, "Write it down." So, I did.

Acknowledgments

James E. Ward Jr.—Thank you for writing your story. Had I not read your book *Zero Victim*, I may never have read *Up from Slavery* and the redemptive story of Booker T. Washington and Tuskegee. Had I not read Booker's writings, this book would not be possible. Though God colored our skin differently, what we have in common is under it. Brother, you have blessed me beyond measure. Roll Tide!

Dana Chandler, Archivist, Tuskegee University—Thank you for the many resources you pointed me to and made available in my three-plus-year Tuskegee journey. Your influence on this project has been priceless. Thank you for introducing me to Charlie Vincent. You and Charlie have had more influence on this project than anyone, outside the grace of God. Without the two of you and your knowledge of history and love for mankind, this project would have never made it out of the blocks. Thank you for your insight and wise counsel. And thank you for introducing me to your friend and colleague Edith Powell.

Edith Powell—Thank you for returning to Tuskegee and immersing yourself in the culture. I appreciate your gracious spirit and willingness to review my manuscript. I cannot begin to express my gratitude for our conversations over the phone. They are always enlightening and enjoyable. Thank you for your love for George Washington Carver and your book *More Than Peanuts*, and for co-writing with Dana Chandler your great work *To Raise Up the Man Farthest Down*. You are truly a woman of the Tuskegee spirit.

Dudley Hall—No words adequately describe how much God has influenced my life because of you. You have taught me how to enjoy God and His amazing grace. How you interpret Scripture through the lens of grace and truth is the gift that keeps on giving, even to a redneck. Your insight in forming a biblical worldview has opened my eyes to keeping the Main Thing the main thing. Thank you, my friend, for loving me through it all. You know the good, the bad, and the ugly, and yet you continue to wrap your arms of grace around me and my family. I am grateful for our little buddy Rawley Curry, who introduced you and Jack Deere to me on a dove field in McCulloch County in 1990. Your wit and ridicule are profound in growing me in the grace of thick skin. You are a treasure.

Charlie Vincent—Thank you for your steadfast support of this project. Your influence on *Critical Grace* has been so rich in knowledge I would not have otherwise, outside of our friendship. Charlie, I am grateful for your willingness to let me into your world to somehow feel the depth of pain your people have endured and continue to endure because you are not White. I said in my book that Booker T. Washington gave me an education in grace. You and Bennie magnify the grace of our Lord, as did Booker. The books and movies you turned me onto were powerful in moving me closer to comprehending the rich gift of lament. Thank you! Thank you! Thank you!

Dr. Margaret Fomer—Since we met last spring at Epic Conference in Carrolton, Texas, you have been an ally to this project. Your willingness to review and edit the manuscript time after time has been a blessing beyond measure. You helped me capture how the words I write will fall on people who don't look like me, and I love you for that. You are my sister and one of my favorite siblings in our kingdom family.

Paul Tripp—Though we have never met, I had to include you because of the influence you have had on my interpretation of grace and mercy. Thank you for speaking truth and grace through *New Morning Mercies*. For the last few years, your daily devotions have become a routine around which Dianne and I begin our days. You are attentive and gifted in hearing the voice of God. How you interpret grace and mercy grows out of your gratitude for the love of Jesus. Anytime I need a good word from grace, I know I can count on you and my good friend Dudley Hall. For the two of you to be my bookends of interpreting grace is a blessing beyond measure.

Philip Barrett—One of my greatest takeaways from my experience in the Chick-fil-A operator selection process was the privilege of getting to know you. Out of that connection came some good times pheasant hunting in South Dakota and antelope hunting in New Mexico. Thank you for prayers and support in our mission at Thriving Oaks. Without that experience, this book would have never become an idea. Most of all, thank you for your friendship. You are a treasured friend.

Kipton Blue—From the day Rick Boxx introduced us, I had a feeling we would become friends. Your appetite for clever sarcasm drew me like a mosquito to a flame. Thank you for your support of me personally and especially for your prayers and support of Thriving Oaks. Without you and Shari and your love for growing the kingdom, this book would not be possible. Thank you for it all—but most of all, thank you for the gift of your grace.

Tim Hogan—My good friend in countless ways. Thank you for the giant handmade arrows you provided for Thriving Oaks and for allowing me to join your team on the set of *The Chosen*, Season 3. I have no doubt God put that diverse group together. We had Black, Hispanic, White, young, and old. Thank you for the many conversations as I was in the "belly of the beast" writing *Critical Grace* during that time. Your love for the Lord flows out of who you are. Grace and mercy flow out of you and your bride, Swan. Thank you for introducing me to A. J. Johnson.

A. J. Johnson—Brother, you became a light in my life from day one when we met working on the set of *The Chosen*, Season 3. Thank you for not discounting the words of a man because he has White skin, and thank you for setting me straight in regard to overcoming fear when speaking the truth, especially in the presence of my siblings who look like you. Thank you for your service as an officer in the Detroit Police Department.

LTC Allen West—You had me at "Booker T. Washington is my ideological mentor." When I heard you speak those words, you became my first choice to write the Foreword of this book. I am grateful our mutual friend, Dudley Hall, introduced us. Thank you for the time you invested to review and critique the manuscript. I am so grateful for how you battle every day for God, your family, and the United States of America. Your *Steadfast & Loyal* podcast has become an important part of my weekly routine. Your tireless love for God and His children inspires me to be a better man. You model excellence as did our friend and mentor, Booker T. Washington.

Marcus White—You my brudda. I cannot tell you how much I appreciate your love and mercy. From the day we served as buddy counselors at Royal Family Kids Camp, you and I have had some fun, and we have had some serious conversations—over succi, of course. I hope we have many years of both on the path ahead. You bless me.

Foster Williams—You are a brother from another mother. I praise God for the thick skin He has graced in you. Our conversations have been so enlightening and a rare blessing between brothers who don't look alike. I remember the day you said to me, "You do Black better than my people." You said that in response to how little your people know about Booker T. Washington. I look forward to more good conversations over lunch after Commissioner's Men.

Ron Rose—Thank you for investing your time to read the manuscript and for your wise counsel in helping me comprehend the value of empathizing with the reader, feeling what a reader may feel as the words pass from the eyes to the mind, then land in the heart. Thank you for over forty years of friendship with you and Lyn. Dianne and I have lots of memories with y'all, and the best ones always involve good food.

Steve Barley—When our buddy Frank Vines introduced us in 1975 on that infamous duck hunt in his new Monte Carlo, we never imagined that fifty years later, we would both be living in the Fort Worth area, working on a book about Booker T. Washington. I appreciate so much your interest in the project from the outset. Thank you for reviewing the many revisions of the manuscript as it evolved into, hopefully, something worth reading. You and Shaun have become two of my favorite people, and Dianne and I look forward to spending eternity with you both.

Keith Long—Thank you for your help in getting my first little book out the door. I will forever be grateful for how you helped me learn how to write and envision where a book is taking the reader. You taught me that you write a chapter, but you build a book. I appreciate your passion for the subject of *Critical Grace*, and for your constant search for resources, articles, etc. that helped move me along in fleshing out something of value for both Blacks and Whites. You and Amy have been a blessing from day one. Thank you for your inspiration and encouragement.

David Holland—Thank you for making this book better. Your skills in knowledge of Scripture and wordsmithery make the light in something I wrote shine a little brighter. Men need men and women need women in our lives that bring out the best and brightest luminance of Christ. You encourage many men, and I am grateful for your influence in my life, personally and through your books, *Praying Grace* and *Grace for Men*.

Bill Rogers—It has been a long friendship since our growing-up days in the sixties in Texarkana. You have a quality that every man longs for. You are the same every day, in a good way. When you won the 1981 British Open, you never changed, and you have remained steadfast and loyal to God, family, friends, and country. And, yes, the game of golf. Thank you for poring over the manuscript and its many changes in the process of becoming *Critical Grace*. You have my greatest admiration, and Dianne and I look forward to spending eternity with y'all.

Tom Avery—Thank you for giving *Critical Grace* an amazingly beautiful first impression. I love the cover which conveys not only the critical nature of grace but also the beauty of the only color that matters, the red blood of our "risen" Lord.

Karen Pickering—Working with you on my first book, *Narrowtive*, was a true pleasure. The same is true of *Critical Grace*. Thank you for your love and care of this project, for making sure that the narrative remained in line with the message that is critical to grace. Thank you for putting up with my annoying ways and my constant need to change and add to the manuscript. No one models grace for my writing like you do, my friend. You are the best.

Tia Smith—Thank you for cleaning up the mess in the manuscript. Your critical eye for detail and care in making it better are greatly appreciated.

No doubt, I have failed to mention someone really important. Grace, please, for my old and growing older memory, and thank you. God knows who you are, and at the end of the day, that's all that really matters. Be blessed.

A book that opens the inner chambers of a people's heart, and sheds a light that may guide the footsteps of both races along the upward way, should meet with a hearty welcome at the hands of all lovers of mankind.
—Booker T. Washington

Introduction

Picture it, my young friends. The clouds of darkness all over the land, black folk and white folk full of fear and hate, wanting to go forward, but each fearful of the other. A whole region is caught in a terrible tension. Everyone is perplexed with the question of what must be done to dissolve this fear and hatred that crouched over the land like a demon waiting to spring.[1]

Sound familiar? Like it came from a current news outlet? Those words were written almost seventy-five years ago in Ralph Ellison's classic novel *Invisible Man.* While Ellison's words are fictional, I have little doubt that he wrote based on his experiences as a student at Tuskegee Institute, only twenty years after the death of Tuskegee's founder, Booker T. Washington. The great stories of Washington—his wisdom, character, magnetic personality, and steadfast love for people of all races—were no doubt still being told while Ellison was a student from 1933 to 1936. It is our loss that the story of Booker T. Washington and Tuskegee, perhaps the greatest story of the invasion of grace on American soil, has grown cold and is no longer being retold.

Until now.

Ellison described the world as he saw it in his day, yet it accurately depicts the cold racial climate and overheated rhetoric we experience today. The racial divide in America has always been troubled waters, but it has grown even more stormy since 2020. The massive disruptions that accompanied the COVID-19 lockdowns frayed our nerves even more. We became agitated about the present and more fearful for what the future holds. We became more suspicious across our society, including all races and all rungs on the economic ladder. The "fear and hatred" Ellison described as "a demon waiting to spring" seemed ready to pounce in full ferocity.

Onto this thick layer of bone-dry underbrush fell the burning sparks and embers of several widely publicized incidents of White police officers using extreme and sometimes deadly methods to subdue Black suspects. The most incendiary of these was the death of George Floyd, fanning the fires of anger and destruction on our streets that had smoldered for decades. The rage unleashed, and the responses to it further polarized us: "Defund the Police versus Back the Blue." One side pointed to gut-wrenching videos; the other to cold data and statistics. All sides pointed the finger of blame. All sides overused and abused the label "racist" until it began to lose all weight or meaning. Mutual condemnation blurred reality. It became a war of words, and frequently more than words. We saw the validity in the old saying "Truth is the first casualty of war." The events and the rhetoric around them magnified our differences, of which the color of our skin remained the most significant difference of all. For those of us old enough to remember the turbulent sixties, it all prompted a terrible sense of déjà vu.

Is it any wonder that discussion of race-related attitudes and relations became more of a "no-go zone" than ever before? The topic of race, which has always been a minefield, is now also a "no-win zone." Even church became a place where healthy discussions regarding race were taboo.

Nevertheless, when we're discussing Christians and churches, we're talking about a people for whom Jesus, in His final hours before the cross, prayed: "That they may all be one, just as You, Father, are in Me, and I in You" (John 17:21). If there were to be any place in America where we should expect to find the courage, compassion, and grace to speak about race in redemptive ways, it would be from our pulpits. But that has not largely been the case.

As a result, Dr. Martin Luther King Jr.'s dream seemed more out of reach than ever. We lost our willingness to identify evil for what it is, filtering everything through the color of our skin rather than the character under it. We lost hope of having peace in our neighborhoods, our schools, our cities, and our country. Even many of our churches were caught up in the fray, blindly following movements that further divided us rather than bearing witness to her identity as the body of Christ and the truth that all lives matter. The truth was being distorted and, in many ways, hidden.

As I witnessed what was going on, I had an uneasiness in the pit of my stomach. While it is good for the church to engage in culture wars, in this case, there seemed to be something amiss and disingenuous: an indifference or fear of getting to the root of why we were so divided. There had to be something we were missing, something or someone in our history that provided a clue to solving our problem of race. I came across a quote from the famous poet and journalist Carl Sandburg that sums up where I believe we are today: "When a society or a civilization perishes, one condition can always be found. They forgot where they came from."[2] The truth is, if our institutions no longer teach us the truth regarding our history, and we no longer retell redemptive stories in our homes, then we have no stories to attach the lessons learned from our ancestors. Until we know the roots of our racial past, we will remain disconnected and divided.

While ignorance of history is common among Blacks and Whites, it is not the case with Native Americans. Native Americans know their history, and as a result, they have a story to tell. They don't write down their stories; they tell and retell the old stories from generation to generation. We cannot remember what we haven't learned or what we haven't been told. The outcome of not knowing our heritage is a major contributor to our current state of unrest. Ignorance of history is an epidemic in America, especially when it comes to knowing there was a time when the divide was shrinking.

Through a journey you will read about in the coming pages, I was reintroduced to Booker T. Washington, whom I had learned about in history class eons ago. I knew he had founded Tuskegee

Institute, was a leader of his race, and had been a colleague of George Washington Carver, but other than that, I was clueless. As I began to ask people what they knew about Booker, I was blown away by the lack of knowledge of this icon in our nation's history. What surprised me the most is how little his own people know about him. That is when I said to myself, *Someone needs to write a book and retell the story of Booker T. Washington and Tuskegee.* In my Tuskegee journey, I discovered that Booker had it going on. He provided everything we need in terms of personal growth, excellence in education, and fostering racial harmony. Booker T. Washington opened the eyes of White America to the brilliance, character, and capabilities possible in an educated man or woman of the Black race. The same can be said of all of us, except today, education has been replaced with indoctrination. Students are being taught what to think and not how.

As I read his writings and the words he spoke, I became convinced that Booker tried to teach both Blacks and Whites how to get along and work together for the benefit of both races. He knew mankind perhaps better than anyone who has gone before us, and he knew the cure for what divides us is in the heart, not in programs, principles, and ministries. What I learned about and from Dr. Washington is that grace is not in winning the argument and that our horizontal afflictions will only be solved vertically. His life lessons have had a profound influence on what I believe about his race as well as mine, and how critical it is that we interpret each other through the lens of grace. When we allow ourselves to see beyond the color of one's skin to the heart under it, something amazing happens. We begin to see that we have more in common than we realize and that our commonality rests in our likeness to Jesus. Tom Huston (who partnered with George Washington Carver in curing many of the early diseases of the peanut) said, "The man within is greater than his skin."[3]

Tuskegee's founder shone light on the path to racial harmony in his day, but he was denied by our ancestors, both Black and White.

Whites denied him because he was Black, and Blacks opposed him
because of the standard of excellence he set for himself and for
his race, plus they could not see the doors of opportunity he had
opened. He called this the "American standard."[4] Booker's solutions
and methods required the long view of life, an organic process
beginning at the bottom, planting roots in the soil of gratitude, and
discovering the joy of a work ethic versus immediate gratification.
Mike Rowe, an American television host and narrator, is right in
saying, "Short cuts lead to long delays." The long delay has gone
on long enough. This was a huge revelation for me, and the more
I thought about it, the more I realized that if we could somehow
begin to retell the story of Booker T. Washington, we just might
rediscover the path to peace he paved. In the process, we could
restore his name to its rightful place of honor as the foremost
educator America has ever known. The answers to just about all of
our problems could well be stored in the archived words of Booker
T. Washington, and in the story of his beloved Tuskegee. Getting
down to "bedrock," as Washington called it, to the foundational
truth, may very well be what we need to calm the troubled waters
of racial anxiety in America.

Booker said, "Character, not circumstances, make the man."[5]
Dr. King echoed Washington's words when he said, "I have a
dream of the day when my four little children will live in a nation
and not be judged by the color of their skin but by the content of
their character."[6] In 1 Corinthians 2:11, the apostle Paul asked the
question: "For what man knows the things of a man except the
spirit of the man which is in him?" The spirit in the heart of a man
or woman is what determines who that person is, not the color of
their skin. The spirit that lived in Booker T. Washington was the
spirit of sonship and not that of a victim. He knew his heritage, and
he knew his destiny.

What Booker accomplished at Tuskegee, interpreting his
race to the world and showing America the beauty and brilliance
his people possessed, was enlightening. At Tuskegee, he showed

us how to educate and build a community, complete in growing hands, heads, and hearts. What he revealed should inspire us all to ascribe to the same, personally and collectively, in our homes, communities, and nation.

Booker chose to love those who opposed him and his race, regardless of the fact that they were White and many were evil. Bedrock to his success was his courage and his high tolerance not to be offended. Booker's mind and heart had thick skin. He never allowed the color of his skin to limit his determination to succeed when others were telling him otherwise. Booker said, "I would permit no man, no matter what his colour might be, to narrow and degrade my soul by making me hate him."[7]

Booker T. Washington discovered the power of grace and forgiveness, and he lived it in a time of oppression and injustice that makes the world today look like a day at the spa. Dr. Washington was more than an emancipated slave; his heart was emancipated. He was committed to loving God, making the most of his wisdom and knowledge, and serving mankind of all races. Dr. Washington was a man of conviction and not consensus. He was the foremost example of a man to be emulated because he was a student of the Bible and lived a life surrendered to Jesus Christ. Getting to know him through his writings has been liberating and, quite honestly, a total joy. Reading Booker T. Washington makes my heart smile. What God has revealed to this old white man through the words of a brilliant man, who happened to be Black and lived over a hundred years ago, has been a blessing beyond measure.

The education I received from Dr. Washington has had the greatest impact on my life of any teaching outside of the Bible. While my knowledge of Dr. Washington and the Tuskegee story grew, the greatest changes evolved under my skin. The transformation of my heart for all races, and especially for my brothers and sisters of the Black race, was not expected nor did I have anything to do with it. If that kind of change can bring peace to the heart of someone like me, it can do the same for others.

As the story of Booker T. Washington became entrenched in my brain, God reminded me of just how important it is that we read and educate ourselves by resurrecting stories from our past, retelling them so we can learn from them and not repeat the same mistakes. Most of the content of *Critical Grace* is from the writings of Booker T. Washington. His words are what make this book worthy of your time. His story and that of Tuskegee are significantly rich in historical accuracy and biblical delight, and in some ways are graciously offensive. For me, this journey from ignorance to knowledge has set me free from myself. It has been a path to peace thanks to what I have learned from the immutable life lessons of Booker T. Washington. You can look forward to attending class taught by Dr. Washington. You will discover not only that he was a gifted educator but that the spirit that flowed out of his heart was seasoned with critical grace. My goal in writing this book is to weave a narrative around Dr. Washington and his legacy of education and racial harmony—and then to weave that narrative into my own story of redemptive grace.

Whether you bought this book or someone gave it to you, thank you. Thank you for caring about this subject of getting along and being friends, regardless of our differences. We are weary individually and as a country, and the voices in the media want to keep us that way. That is why you and I must educate ourselves, our families, and our friends. We must educate our church leaders to stand in the gap for God and face the culture wars as we are called to do as the body of Christ. If the church cannot be depended upon to be the voice of God to a depraved and suffering world, and to inject the values and virtues of Jesus Christ into the political arena, who will be?

You will not read about DEI, affirmative action programs, principles, or ministries to do this or that for a solution to our divide. We have done just about everything known to man—most of it wrong—to mandate racial equality. Actor Denzel Washington summed it up perfectly when he said, "You can't legislate love."[8]

What I learned from Booker T. Washington is that justice, whether racial or of another kind, is an "inside job," and only there, by the grace of God, will we be united under God.

The subject of race is uncomfortable. It is so for Blacks, for Whites, for Native Americans, and for every other race and ethnicity. It is possibly the most effective weapon the enemy of God uses against us to keep us divided. Satan is active, relentless, and effective in destroying us from the inside because of what we look like on the outside. My hope is that *Critical Grace* will provide something to help you disarm the source of evil and open the door to a quieter Spirit, leading to a calmer life of peace. My heartfelt desire is for you to live with less anxiety and to be a little easier on yourself and those you live and work with, for the streets of America to become civilized again, and for our kids and grandkids to live in a friendlier and more respectful environment where race gives way to grace. When our hearts are integrated with the love of Jesus, peace will be restored in our homes, in our schools, and on our streets. God sees us from the inside out. By His grace, we can do the same. That is grace, and it is critical.

In the words of Brennan Manning, "All is grace."[9]

PART I

Revelation Grace

Education in the broadest and truest sense will make an individual seek to help all people, regardless of race, regardless of colour, regardless of condition. And you will find that the person who is most truly educated is the one who is going to be kindest, and is going to act in the gentlest manner toward persons who are unfortunate.
—Booker T. Washington

CHAPTER ONE

Lifting the Veil of Ignorance

We live in this bubble of ignorance. Most people know nothing about history, or the historical context of the traditions they still follow today. People do things without knowing why they're doing them.
—Oliver Markus Malloy

Sam was forty-two, had a college degree, and was in his twelfth year as a firefighter. He was smart, but intellect would not be considered his strongest quality. He had a beautiful wife of sixteen years and two children: a son, fifteen, and a daughter, twelve. Sam loved the outdoors, and he enjoyed sports, especially March Madness. But Sam was different from many men in that he loved to read. He hadn't always been a reader, but reading had become Sam's friend in the quieter moments at the firehouse. Sam enjoyed a good novel but loved to read about history, autobiographies, and stories of the great men and women who made the world around them better.

After the death of George Floyd, Sam's church was attempting to solve the problem of racism, encouraging people to enroll in classes to learn about White supremacy, White fragility, and systemic racism and to support the Black Lives Matter movement. There was even a class for Whites on how to speak the language of Blacks, which Sam thought was absurd. He'd always believed the way you talk to people is with respect and dignity, regardless of who they are or the color of their skin. The church staff further encouraged families to march in BLM protests and to support defunding those who serve and protect us from the bad guys. That's when Sam said to himself, *This is wrong*. Sam's church was historically known for its "open to anyone" fellowship, but for some reason, during the outcry for racial justice, she drifted from her identity as the body of Christ to lean into the popular rhetoric of guilt and shame being voiced on the streets. Something just didn't add up, and Sam sensed it. He couldn't put his finger on it right off, but he was convinced there was something amiss regarding racism that was not being told, or maybe it was simply ignorance.

At the same time, Sam had some concerns regarding what was going on in the school system. Sam's children attended a school that had just hired a new coach/teacher. Coach Marcus was hired as an assistant football coach and would also teach PE and American History. Because Coach Marcus was Black, he was also assigned the responsibility of overseeing the newly added DEI programs, including a student-led diversity council. Also, the school board had recently okayed transgender boys competing in girls' sports, opening the door for boys in the girls' locker room. There was so much going on in Sam's world that just didn't make sense, and it was not sitting well. To Sam, it was "madness." What was happening in the world? Why were the leaders in our country, our community, our schools, and our churches following ideologies that made no sense? Sam had no answer. Do you?

While the name in this story is fictitious, the story itself is being played out every day in communities all across America in one way or another. Sam's concern for his family, his kids' school, and their church are real and are not unique to Sam. More than likely, you are witnessing a similar case of misguided leadership promoting destructive ideologies in your community. The truth is, we shouldn't be surprised. We live in a fallen world with an enemy that wants to steal, kill, and destroy anything that God created, including you and me. The current path the United States of America is on is one of destruction. We have allowed our educators to become indoctrinators, and we are paying a heavy price for the kind of adults our sons and daughters are becoming in a world that needs for them to be mature, confident, and law-loving citizens. Our schools no longer educate and train future adults for a life of purpose, and the church remains silent in these realities, as it did in Nazi Germany in the thirties and forties.

It was Christmas, and Sam's daughter, knowing her dad loved to read, gave him a copy of Booker T. Washington's *Up from Slavery*. From the moment Sam opened and began to read, he was drawn in. He couldn't put it down, and before long Sam discovered the value of the book he held—that it could very well possess the cure for our racial chasm and much more. Sam concluded that the story of Booker T. Washington and Tuskegee is not just an idea that could restore America but is *the* idea, *the* solution, and *the* cure for what divides us.

If we had educated our children the Booker T. Washington way, you wouldn't be reading this book because there would be no need for it. There would be peace in our homes, in our schools, and on our streets. That's water under the bridge now, yet Booker's writings hold the key to getting us back to being a nation of the educated versus the indoctrinated. I cannot emphasize enough that this is *the* way back. I know this to be true because, like Sam, I too picked up a copy of *Up from Slavery*, and the education I received from Booker T. Washington has been a transforming experience. Booker T. Washington gave America the exact template for education and character development. What he taught and how he taught it was— and is—essential to a well-lived life and a civilized America. Isn't that what we all desire for ourselves and for our sons and daughters?

Folks, we are in a civil war, not unlike the kind that Booker T. Washington experienced in his youth. The civil war that has been brewing and is raging today is the battle for control of our minds and our hearts. Either we are civil toward God or we are not. Every one of the institutions of our land is in peril because of the broken world we live in. It is fixable, but not horizontally. While the brokenness is horizontal, the solutions are vertical. This was true in the days of Booker T. Washington, and it is true today. The difference is Booker T. Washington figured out early on that there were great opportunities for him, for the people of his race, and for high-minded Whites. If the people of his race were going to succeed in America, he knew it was going to take working together with White people,. He also knew it would require perhaps the most challenging and uncomfortable action known to man: forgiveness. Booker T. Washington knew that forgiveness was the environment of God, and it was bedrock to the success of his race in a world controlled by Whites. Forgiveness and the amazing grace of God were critical to Booker T. Washington's success, and the candle he lit at Tuskegee, though it has grown dim, can still shine today.

What Booker T. Washington accomplished at Tuskegee Institute not only gave us a template to follow, it was the manifestation of himself and the excellence by which he lived. Tuskegee became known among educators worldwide as *the* model to follow. The following words from Dr. Washington describe how students at Tuskegee were educated and will give you a peek into why Tuskegee flourished under the leadership of Booker T. Washington.

> They are being taught that mind-training is the logical helpmeet of hand-training, and that both, supplemented and sweetened by heart-training, make the high-souled, useful, productive, patriotic, law-loving, public-spirited citizen, of whom any nation might well be proud. The outcome of such education will be that, instead of the downtrodden child of ignorance, shiftlessness, and moral weakness, we shall generate the thoroughly rounded man of prudence, foresight, responsibility, and financial independence. He will cease to be the gullible victim of the sharper who plays upon vanity,

credulity, and superstition, and learn to value only
that which is real and substantial.[1]

Need I say more? Though the messenger is long gone, the light
of Booker T. Washington can be refueled to shine brighter than ever
in a dark and depraved world. But it must first shine in my heart
and yours. The light of forgiveness leads to success and according
to Dr. Washington, "Success is to be measured not so much by the
position that one has reached in life as by the obstacles which he
has overcome while trying to succeed."[2] Every way the enemy of
God attacks us is an obstacle, which includes our differences, racial
and otherwise. That same light of forgiveness can shine in you and
me, but we must choose to light the flame. The candle of grace that
glowed in the heart of Booker T. Washington shone in a time that
was ugly, one we would like to forget as though it never happened.
We were bad, but we were in the process of becoming better. Booker
T. Washington was vital to the progress of the process, and that
process continues today. We were better for a time but have allowed
the world around us to grow even darker than in the days of Booker
T. Washington. The candle of grace will shine again when we make
the choice to let it shine together. It will shine again in our country,
in our government, in our schools, and in our homes, but only when
it shines first in you and me. Let's light this candle together.

*Institutions, like individuals, are properly judged by their ideals, their
methods, and their achievements in the production of men and women
who are to do the world's work.*
—Booker T. Washington

The Journey Begins

So how did I become interested in a man who lived over a hundred
years ago, who happened to be Black? I'm glad you asked. The short
answer is "only by the grace of God." That is literally the only answer

I have. I was searching online for a publisher for my first book, *Narrowtive*, and was drawn to a prospective publisher's listing of a book written by James E. Ward Jr. The title *Zero Victim: Overcoming Injustice with a New Attitude* seemed interesting, so I ordered a copy. I had no idea how this book was going to begin a process that would ultimately transform my heart.

In his book, Pastor Ward shared how he scored a zero on a test to quantify how you view yourself as a victim. The test was given to the staff of the church where he served, and the people administering the test were perplexed by Pastor Ward's result. In his book, he told the story of his life and how he came to embody such confidence and not allow his circumstances to create in him a victimhood mentality. It is a great story that goes deep in helping us comprehend the battle for our hearts that takes place in our minds. To quote Pastor Ward:

> A Zero Victim mentality is the solution to respond-ing to injustice in society. A Zero Victim mentality empowers potential victims to rise above anger, in-sult, or unforgiveness toward those who initiated injustices against them, with a new attitude. This mindset prevents the recipient of injustice from pointing the finger of blame toward others and changes their perspective about it.[3]

Pastor Ward dug deep into the influences that build our self-confidence. He wrote about the men and women who spoke truth in his life. One of the men he highly respected and considered a source of inspiration was Booker T. Washington. Pastor Ward said this regarding Washington:

> Like any other human born into such conditions, Booker T. could easily justify victimization in his own thinking. He received no schooling as a slave,

yet he was known to be forward-thinking in his perspectives in life. Despite the hardships black Americans faced, Booker T. embraced a Zero Victim mindset and believed blacks could rise above every challenge they faced.[4]

Pastor Ward's description of Booker T. Washington captured my attention. He wrote about Washington's autobiography *Up from Slavery*, so I ordered a copy. As I read it, something I never expected began to take hold of me. The more I read, the more I realized the Booker's writings, his words of wisdom and immutable truth, need to be read and shared by every American. Booker's writings are the bedrock to lifting the veil of our ignorance. The entire book is a lesson in history, a manual for personal growth, and a tool for teaching character to our children, and most of all, it proves that life is not about me. And he managed to write with an overtone of racial harmony. If I had to choose one big hook that kept me on the line of Booker's rod and reel of enlightenment, it was this: everything he wrote over a century ago remains relevant today.

> As I read it, something I never expected began to take hold of me.

Up from Slavery is Booker T. Washington's story of how, in spite of being born into slavery, he eventually became a university president. His influence was profound as an adviser to world leaders, including four U.S. presidents. As I read and learned more, I became somewhat disappointed that I had never heard Washington's story before. Yes, I knew who Booker T. Washington was and that he had founded Tuskegee Institute. But the rest of his story—the details, the good stuff, the takeaways—had somehow remained hidden until I read about them in Booker's autobiography. Through this process, I discovered just how important it is that we read, retell, and learn from our history.

I was struck by the truths regarding his oppression and suffering and was in awe of his victories. I was amazed by the men and women who influenced him, as well as the influence he had on his students and the staff at Tuskegee. He touched the communities surrounding Tuskegee and Macon County, Alabama. All of this was new to me. He was no ordinary man, and Tuskegee is no ordinary place.

> The details, the good stuff, had somehow evaded me for most of my life.

This new information ignited a fire in me to know more—not just for me, but for my adult children, my grandchildren, and my friends. I had to share the story of Booker T. Washington—how he rose from the bottom of human existence to a place of prominence as a student, father, university president, respected leader, and, most of all, a man who knew who he was, his purpose, and his destiny. I am blessed that my veil of ignorance is being lifted day by day in my continuing education from Booker T. Washington. Education is so underrated in the world today, yet it remains essential to progress as an individual and collectively as a nation. Nelson Mandela said this about education:

> Education is the great engine of personal development. It is through education that the daughter of a peasant can become a doctor, that the son of a mineworker can become the head of the mine, that a child of farm workers can become the president of a great nation. It is what we make out of what we have, not what we are given, that separates one person from another.[5]

I was hooked by the story of Booker T. Washington, so much so that I reached out to Tuskegee University to learn more. My appetite to learn more about Booker was insatiable, and eventually I was introduced to university archivist Dana Chandler. Understandably, Dana was somewhat apprehensive in our first phone conversation as he listened to me describe my book idea. He suggested I order the book *To Raise Up the Man Farthest Down*, which he cowrote with Edith Powell. Mrs. Powell taught at Tuskegee University for thirty years, and Dana has been archivist for eighteen years. Their book is an account of the medical contributions and advancements that came about as a result of research conducted at Tuskegee.

> He created a thriving environment of excellence in every category.

I came to realize just how brilliant Booker T. Washington was, as were the men and women he invited to join him at Tuskegee. He created a thriving environment of excellence in every category, especially in the fields of medicine and agriculture. To this day the world benefits from the fruit of the discoveries made at Tuskegee.

The first time I was able to meet with Dana, we began to get to know each other and build trust. As we talked, we discovered some common ground—we both grew up in the Church of Christ, and we both like to hunt and fish. As we continued in conversation, it became apparent we have kindred hearts and a love for people, especially people of color. The meeting went well, and I left with some good resource material. We scheduled a second meeting, and Dana continued to provide insight and information vital to the content in this book.

In the process of having my ignorance unveiled, God opened my eyes to the reality of the magnitude of what was accomplished at Tuskegee, and how His grace was poured out on Booker, his staff, the students of Tuskegee Institute, the Black race, and the world. Some of what you read may be hard to hear, but hopefully, the blessings will far outweigh the discomfort. Discovering the deeper truths of God's grace has been liberating for me while learning and retelling the story of Tuskegee. My heart was becoming emancipated from the bondage of myself, and I didn't realize it until well into the journey. While freedom from myself was the outcome personally, I believe God had another purpose. I believe He called me to enlighten His children with Black skin about one of their own, whom He chose to speak grace through in a moment in time.

> *God is going to reveal to us things*
> *He never revealed before if we put our*
> *hands in His.*
> —George Washington Carver

CHAPTER TWO

Who Was Booker Taliaferro Washington?

*He is a man who, in every sense, deserves well of his contemporaries
and I believe that, when hereafter the story is written
of Christian people's endeavor in our day to atone for
and to amend the racial wrongdoing of the past,
Mr. Booker T. Washington's name will stand in the
very forefront of those for whom the world will give thanks.*
—The Archbishop of Canterbury

The following words were spoken by Booker T. Washington's successor, Robert Russa Moton, in an address given in New York City, honoring Dr. Washington in 1915, the year following his passing. Like Washington, Moton was a friend of humanity and would later be named the keynote speaker at the dedication of the Lincoln Memorial in 1922. His words are a fitting introduction of Booker T. Washington, how he lived and was loved, revered, and  respected throughout the world, in America, and especially in his beloved Alabama.

At the very simple but impressive funeral service at
Tuskegee, in November, more than eight thousand
people—rich and poor, from city and country,
educated and uneducated, from North and South,
black and white—gathered to pay reverently their
last tribute of respect and devotion to the man they
loved. The beautiful city of Tuskegee, by special
request of its honored Mayor, ceased all business
during the funeral hour. Practically every white
business house and organization, together with
hundreds of individuals in Tuskegee and Macon
County, as well as throughout the great State of
Alabama (to say nothing about the colored people),
sent floral offerings, and to a Negro, mind you! And
this, my friends, was in the shadow, almost, of the
old Confederate capitol in Montgomery. Alabama
and the South loved Booker Washington; Booker
Washington loved Alabama and the South, where
he lived, labored, and died, and where he wanted
to be buried.[1]

Booker T. Washington was a man who feared God, read daily
from His Word, and lived with a forgiving spirit. He was revered by
the poor as well as leaders of the free world. He allowed himself to
be influenced by the character of God and by those he encountered
throughout his life. He noticed people and learned from those
who lived with high morals and character and who valued the
development of good habits. He also learned what to avoid from
those who lived life to serve themselves.

While living on a plantation, young Washington took a job
working in the home of General Lewis Ruffner, the owner of the
coal and salt mine where he had been working with his brother. He
had heard how demanding Mrs. Ruffner was from the boys who
worked for her, but young Booker was determined to take the job

because he wanted out of the dismal environment of working in the coal and salt mine. Young Washington was somewhat apprehensive as he began to work for Mrs. Ruffner. However, in short order, he came to understand her, what she expected, and she was pleased with everything about him. He was honest, hard-working, and always went above and beyond what was expected of him. Not only did he do a good job, he had an ethic of completing any task he was assigned. Booker T. Washington and Mrs. Ruffner became friends, and she had a major influence on him personally and on his growing heart, as he was preparing to pursue an education at Hampton Institute.

After living on the street, spending most nights sleeping on the ground under the wooden-slat sidewalks, young Washington would go to Hampton Institute every day and attempt to be enrolled. Hampton was a school run by high-character White people for the purpose of educating men and women of the Black race as well as Native Americans.

> Perhaps the thing that touched and pleased me most in connection with my starting for Hampton was the interest that many of the older coloured people took in the matter. They had spent the best days of their lives in slavery, and hardly expected to live to see the time when they would see a member of their race leave home to attend a boarding-school. Some of these older people would give me a nickel, others a quarter, or a handkerchief.[2]

Higher Learning

Once granted admission to Hampton Institute, his interactions with fellow students and teachers reinforced the value of serving others. He recognized he was blessed, and he was acknowledged by others for his special gifts of acquiring knowledge and influencing others. His reputation as a quality student rapidly grew. He became a leader and a man of high character.

> He exposed himself to men and women who lived to serve others.

Dr. Washington's experience at Hampton was an adventure into a new world. Having meals at regular hours, eating on a tablecloth, and having a bathtub and toothbrush were all new to him. While he was getting an education, he exposed himself to men and women who lived to serve others. They made a life-changing impression on him. In his words . . .

No one seemed to think of himself. And the officers and teachers, what a rare set of human beings they were! They worked for the students night and day, in season and out of season. They seemed happy only when they were helping the students in some manner. Whenever it is written—and I hope it will be—the part that the Yankee teachers played in the education of the Negroes immediately after the war will make one of the most thrilling parts of the history of this country.[3]

> Humility and a heart of gratitude
> are key to a lifestyle of power-filled rest.
> —David Holland, Praying Grace for Men

Dr. Washington continued to thrive at Hampton, largely due to the individuals who provided opportunities to maximize his potential. One of those was Miss Mary F. Mackie, the lady principal who first admitted him. He described her influence . . .

It was hard for me at this time to understand how a woman of her education and social standing could take such delight in performing such service, in order to assist in the elevation of an unfortunate race. Ever since then I have had no patience with any school for my race in the South which did not teach its students the dignity of labour. . . .

At Hampton I not only learned that it was not a disgrace to labour, but learned to love labour, not alone for its financial value, but for labour's own sake and for the independence and self-reliance which the ability to do something which the world wants done brings. At that institution I got my first taste of what it meant to live a life of unselfishness, my first knowledge of the fact that the happiest individuals are those who do the most to make others useful and happy.[4]

In Washington's second year at Hampton, he was introduced to the Bible. The value of the Bible was his most critical experience that year. It was at Hampton where he developed the habit of reading daily from the Word. As his knowledge of the Bible grew, he began to see that God had a plan and purpose for his life. The ascension from being the man farthest down had begun.

After Booker graduated from Hampton Institute, he was given the opportunity to continue his education in Washington, DC. While there, General Samuel Chapman Armstrong, the founder of Hampton Institute, invited him to return to Hampton to mentor young Native Americans. This profoundly illustrates who Booker was becoming and how gracious he was toward his fellow man, regardless of their ethnicity.

> I found that they were about like any other human beings; that they responded to kind treatment and resented ill-treatment.

General Armstrong was the son of missionaries in Hawaii and was a leader in the education of non-Whites.

General Armstrong selected Booker T. Washington to mentor young Native Americans because he knew Washington was up to the task and embodied absolutely no racial prejudice. Washington spoke of his experience:

> About this time the experiment was being tried for the first time, by General Armstrong, of educating Indians at Hampton. Few people then had any confidence in the ability of the Indians to receive education and to profit by it. General Armstrong was anxious to try the experiment systematically on a large scale. He secured from the reservations in the Western states over one hundred wild and for the most part perfectly ignorant Indians, the greater proportion of whom were young men. The special work which the General desired me to do was to be a sort of "house father" to the Indian young men— that is, I was to live in the building with them and have the charge of their discipline, clothing, rooms, and so on. This was a very tempting offer, but I had become so much absorbed in my work in West Virginia that I dreaded to give it up. However, I tore myself away from it. I did not know how to refuse to perform any service that General Armstrong desired of me.
>
> On going to Hampton, I took up my residence in a building with about seventy-five Indian youths. I was the only person in the building who was not a member of their race. At first I had a good deal of doubt about my ability to succeed. I knew that the average Indian felt himself above the white man, and, of course, he felt himself far above the

Negro, largely on account of the fact of the Negro having submitted to slavery—a thing which the Indian would never do. The Indians, in the Indian Territory, owned a large number of slaves during the days of slavery. Aside from this, there was a general feeling that the attempt to educate and civilize the red men at Hampton would be a failure. All this made me proceed very cautiously, for I felt keenly the great responsibility. But I was determined to succeed. It was not long before I had the complete confidence of the Indians, and not only this, but I think I am safe in saying that I had their love and respect. I found that they were about like any other human beings; that they responded to kind treatment and resented ill-treatment. They were continually planning to do something that would add to my happiness and comfort. The things that they disliked most, I think, were to have their long hair cut, to give up wearing their blankets, and to cease smoking; but no white American ever thinks that any other race is wholly civilized until he wears the white man's clothes, eats the white man's food, speaks the white man's language, and professes the white man's religion. . . .

It was a constant delight to me to note the interest which the coloured students took in trying to help the Indians in every way possible. . . .

I have often wondered if there was a white institution in this country whose students would have welcomed the incoming of more than a hundred companions of another race in the cordial way that these black students at Hampton welcomed the red ones. How often I have wanted to say to white students that they lift themselves up in proportion as they help to lift others, and the more unfortunate the race, and the lower in the scale of civilization, the more does one raise one's self by giving the assistance. . . .

My experience has been that the time to test a true gentleman is to observe him when he is in contact with individuals of a race that is less fortunate than his own. This is illustrated in no better way than by observing the conduct of the old-school type of Southern gentleman when he is in contact with his former slaves or their descendants. . . .

While I was in charge of the Indian boys at Hampton, I had one or two experiences which illustrate the curious workings of caste in America.[5]

Cast Down Your Bucket Where You Are

Booker was known for his drive, always in pursuit of accomplishing something versus merely talking about what needed to be done. Booker said that to be successful in any kind of undertaking, the main thing is for one to grow to the point where he completely forgets himself; that is, to lose himself in a great cause. He was invited by the Honorary Thomas W. Bicknell to deliver an address to the Educational Association in Madison, Wisconsin, where around four thousand people were present when Booker spoke. This was the beginning of his public speaking career.

> Anything that I attempted to do for the members of my own race would be of no real value to them unless it was of equal value to the members of the white race by whom they were surrounded.[6]

In Madison, Booker did not know, but there were a large number of White people present from Alabama, specifically from the Tuskegee area. Afterward, these people told Washington they were surprised to hear no words of abuse in his address. This was the first speech Booker gave that dealt in a general sense with the problem of race. Those who heard it seemed to be pleased with what they heard and the general position he took.

> It is hard to convert an individual by abusing him.

Booker was committed to never saying anything in a public address in the North that he wasn't willing to say in the South. He'd learned early on that it is hard to convert an individual by abusing him. A wiser path gives credit for praiseworthy actions rather than calling attention to evil ones. In this address at Madison, Dr. Washington's narrative continued to seek to unite Blacks and Whites, and to encourage the cultivation of friendly relations between the races instead of creating agitation and division. He put it this way:

> In my early life I used to cherish a feeling of ill will toward any one who spoke in bitter terms against the Negro, or who advocated measures that tended to oppress the black man or take from him opportunities for growth in the most complete manner. Now, whenever I hear any one advocating measures that are meant to curtail the development of another, I pity the individual who would do this. I know that the one who makes this mistake does so because of his own lack of opportunity for the highest kind of growth. I pity him because I know that he is trying to stop the progress of the world, and because I know that in time the development

and the ceaseless advance of humanity will make him ashamed of his weak and narrow position. One might as well try to stop the progress of a mighty railroad train by throwing his body across the track, as to try to stop the growth of the world in the direction of giving mankind more intelligence, more culture, more skill, more liberty, and in the direction of extending more sympathy and more brotherly kindness."[7]

The address in Madison was an introduction of Booker T. Washington to the North, and it opened the door for more invitations for him to speak. But he had his eyes on the bigger picture, recalling, "I was anxious, however, that the way might also be opened for me to speak directly to a representative Southern white audience."[8] The first invitation of this kind presented itself in 1893, at the international meeting of the Christian Workers, which was held in Atlanta.

The opportunity to speak in Atlanta presented two distinct challenges. First, Booker was scheduled to be in Boston prior to the scheduled speech, so it would require a great deal of planning to pull off arriving in Atlanta at the appointed time. Second, one of the stipulations was that his speech not go over five minutes. He wondered if he would be able to put enough into a five-minute speech to justify him making such a trip. He knew that the audience in Atlanta would be largely composed of the most influential class of White men and women, and that it would be a rare opportunity for

> He was the first Black man invited to share the stage with Whites.

him to share about the big plans at Tuskegee. He decided to make the trip and spoke for five minutes. The audience of two thousand people was comprised mostly of Whites from both the South and the North. He received a favorable review in the Atlanta newspapers the next day.

Although it was a difficult trip to Atlanta for a five-minute speech, Booker T. Washington rarely, if ever, chose the convenient route, always choosing to do the right thing instead. Because he made the choice to accept the invitation to speak, he was rewarded with an invitation to speak again in Atlanta two years later. This time he would be speaking to a larger audience at the Atlanta Cotton States and International Exposition in 1895. He was the first Black man invited to share the stage with Whites. The opening two paragraphs of his speech were powerful, and those words were essential to the heart transplant taking place in me.

> A ship lost at sea for many days suddenly sighted a friendly vessel. From the mast of the unfortunate vessel was seen a signal, "Water, water; we die of thirst!" The answer from the friendly vessel at once came back, "Cast down your bucket where you are." A second time the signal, "Water, water; send us water!" ran up from the distressed vessel, and was answered, "Cast down your bucket where you are." And a third and fourth signal for water was answered, "Cast down your bucket where you are." The captain of the distressed vessel, at last heeding the injunction, cast down his bucket, and it came up full of fresh, sparkling water from the mouth of the Amazon River. To those of my race who depend on bettering their condition in a foreign land or who underestimate the importance of cultivating friendly relations with the Southern white man, who is their next-door neighbour, l would say: "Cast down your bucket where you are"—cast it down in making friends in every manly way of the people of all races by whom we are surrounded.

Cast it down in agriculture, mechanics, in commerce, in domestic service, and in the professions. And in this connection, it is well to bear in mind that whatever other sins the South may be called to bear, when it comes to business, pure and simple, it is in the South that the Negro is given a man's chance in the commercial world, and in nothing is this Exposition more eloquent than in emphasizing this chance. Our greatest danger is that in the great leap from slavery to freedom we may overlook the fact that the masses of us are to live by the productions of our hands, and fail to keep in mind that we shall prosper in proportion as we learn to dignify and glorify common labour and put brains and skill into the common occupations of life; shall prosper in proportion as we learn to draw the line between the superficial and the substantial, the ornamental gewgaws of life and the useful. No race can prosper till it learns that there is as much dignity in tilling a field as in writing a poem. It is at the bottom of life we must begin, and not at the top. Nor should we permit our grievances to overshadow our opportunities.[9]

I read Booker's seven powerful words—"cast your bucket down where you are"—about the same time I was seeing a counselor who was helping me unpack some of the baggage I've carried since I was a kid. That phrase helped me to realize I had never viewed life from the bedrock truth that life is not about me. Booker was teaching that life is better when we cast down our bucket where we are and live life content in each moment. When we come to grips with the truth that life is about serving God and those around us, we can live free from what and who makes us crazy—"ourselves." John Piper said it simply: "God is most glorified in us when we are most satisfied in Him."[10] When we cast down our bucket where we are, we allow our internal pursuits to follow a humbler and more benevolent path in the process of life, creating contentment. Because of what Jesus did on the cross, God provides all we need to be content with who we are and where God has placed us in the world. We can be at peace with Him, our family, our vocation, and ourselves. And, yes, we can be at peace with each other, regardless of the color of our skin and all the other ways God's enemy keeps us divided.

In his speech at the Cotton States and International Exposition, Booker spoke directly to his people, but also to those of the White race, in a convicting yet delightful delivery. To his people, Booker exhorted them to recognize the opportunities available in the growing South. To the White race, he called attention to the value of making educational opportunities available to the Black race and to the success that was possible when the two races lived and worked together.

Later in his message, Booker spoke of how his people had proven their loyalty to White people in the past, in nursing the children of White families on the plantations, in sitting by sickbeds with mothers and fathers, and often in following them with tear-dimmed eyes to the graves of family members. He went on to say,

> In the future, in our humble way, we shall stand by you with a devotion that no foreigner can approach, ready to lay down our lives, if need be, in defense of yours, interlacing our industrial, commercial, civil, and religious life with yours in a way that shall make the interests of both races one. In all things that are purely social we can be as separate as the fingers, yet one as the hand in all things essential to mutual progress.[11]

The Black race has indeed laid down her life in defense of White people in every war America has engaged in, fighting side by side to protect the freedoms too long denied once they returned home.

Booker continued to speak with a spirit of racial harmony, and the demands for public addresses increased. These invitations came in about equal numbers from his own race and from Northern Whites. Most of his addresses in the North were related to raising funds for Tuskegee. The messages to his own people primarily focused on impressing upon them the importance of industrial and technical education, in addition to academic and religious training

Booker called people of all races to a higher standard—when both conducting business and serving—because of the standard by which he lived. He chose his words wisely to encourage a spirit of progress and unity. He spoke to White people in a respectful yet challenging tone, proposing that they would serve better and be better served when they cast down their buckets among the people of his race. He reminded Whites of how his people had been loyal workers and made the case that if Whites would encourage Blacks in education of hands, head, and heart, they and their families would be surrounded by patient, faithful, law-abiding, and unresentful people.

This is the tone we need from those leading our country today instead of one that agitates, nourishes a spirit of bitterness, and feeds on the victimhood mentality. To be patient, faithful, law-abiding, and unresentful are all qualities Booker embodied. Just think how different our world would be if the leaders of both races had built on those virtues instead of being led to believe they are victims and should live depending on others for their livelihood? As horrific as the bondage of slavery was in those days, the oppression of laws intended to help has created a culture of dependence on the government for too many people. This is oppression of a different kind. Education and opportunities for self-reliance are the path to peace and prosperity. The answer is not what someone else can do for you. The answer is within each one of us. We are so much more than the sum total of our brokenness. Jesus made it so.

Dr. Washington laid the path for a better civilization for people of all races, but especially for the people of his race and underprivileged Whites. Stories of Booker T. Washington, George Washington Carver, and other men of character from our past must be retold so we can learn from mistakes made in the past and build on that knowledge. Reading and educating ourselves lifts the veil of ignorance and opens our minds to healthier relationships, regardless of the color of our skin.

> Dr. Washington laid the path for a better civilization for people of all races.

Booker T. Washington called both races to a higher standard, simply by casting down our bucket wherever we are. He cast his bucket down as the son of a slave. He cast it down in his pursuit of an education at Hampton Institute and in mentoring young Native Americans. He cast it down as founder and president of Tuskegee Institute, and he cast his bucket down among his staff, American presidents, and world leaders. In each moment where he had been placed by the sovereignty of God, he was present.

Over the last couple of years, I have often thought about Booker's speech and his words to "cast down your bucket where you are." These seven words became relevant to me when God revealed that I had never truly cast down my bucket, which means acknowledging the sovereignty of God and being content where He has placed me. Author Henri Nouwen said, "A seed only flourishes by staying in the ground in which it is sown."[12]

"Cast down your bucket where you are" revealed to me the true meaning of embracing the sovereignty of God and making peace with myself in the process, in the place and time God has placed me. As I took everything off the calendar and began weeding out nonessential goings and doings, my heart was in the process of being transformed to fewer self-centered pursuits. Yes, my hunting and fishing have been curtailed to a large degree. I still love the feel of my Beretta 20 gauge and my Thomas and Thomas fly rod, but my heart is in a different place, with a peace like I have never experienced before. To be honest, I can thank Booker T. Washington for revealing so many truths about myself. I have wondered why it has taken so many years for God to set me free from myself, and then it occurred to me that we all have a starting point in the process of becoming who God designed us to be. I think I have always been in a slower class; you know. Like Buddy in *Elf*, a "cotton-headed ninny-muggins."[13] It has just taken me longer to discover the realities of God's grace. Having my eyes opened to the fact that life is not about me and beginning to live like I believed it has been perhaps my greatest discovery under the tutelage of Professor Washington. It is by grace that God has set me free from myself through what I have learned from the mistakes and sinfulness of my past. Washington's words "cast down your bucket where you are" have had a major influence on the transformation of my heart.

> I am at peace and am enjoying life more than ever.

The greatest outcome of casting down my bucket is the impact it has had on my marriage. I don't think I ever really knew how to be married. I know that sounds strange, coming from someone who has been married for over fifty years and professes to be a Christian. But Dianne and I had, like so many couples, grown tolerant of each other. She did her thing; I did mine—all the while allowing our friendship to grow cold. As I stayed home more, we began to enjoy each other's company again. For the first time in my life, I can honestly say that I am at peace and am enjoying life more than ever. Dianne and her gracious heart are, and have always been, the centerpiece of our home. The psalmist described Dianne perfectly: "Your wife shall be like a fruitful vine in the very heart of your house, your children like olive plants all around your table" (Psalm 128:3).

These seven words spoken by Booker T. Washington over a hundred years ago are relevant today, for every one of us. They are relevant personally, and they are relevant collectively, as a nation. They exhort you to be content in God's sovereign will wherever He places you in life. Like me, you can discover the opportunities around you—and more importantly, the people around you. In the process, God has revealed the greater beauty of loving my family as much as I have always loved my friends. That may sound strange, but when you think about it, we are all guilty of it. We are kinder and easier to be around in the presence of those outside our family. Becoming aware of this affliction was an eye-opener for this old idiot.

The power of those seven words spoken in Atlanta in 1895 ring ever true today. Booker articulated his thoughts as encouragement for all races, yet courageously spoke them in a world controlled by White people. His example of courageous faith and commitment to forgiveness and grace could only be divinely orchestrated. Think of where America might be today if our culture was in agreement with Booker's selfless approach to our individual responsibility

His legacy just might be our path to peace.

of education and character development. Where would America be, where would you and I be, had people of both races heeded Washington's call to "cast down your bucket where you are"?

Booker T. Washington faced each day with a spirit of forgiveness in pursuit of the heart of God. Wherever he was, he was present in that moment. His heart was full of gratitude and grace, which was conveyed in how he valued relationships and demonstrated in each opportunity that came his way. People loved that about him, and if you and I choose to become more like Booker, who knows, they might even like us better—and wouldn't that be a good thing to begin the process of becoming a more useful and distinguished citizen?

> *It is not hyperbole to say that Booker T. Washington*
> *was a great American. For twenty years before his death he had been*
> *the most useful, as well as the most distinguished, member of his race*
> *in the world, and one of the most useful, as well as one of the most*
> *distinguished, of American citizens of any race.*
> —Theodore Roosevelt

The Man Farthest Down

To Raise Up the Man Farthest Down by Dana Chandler and Edith Powell is a historical account of the little-known role Tuskegee Institute played in medical advancements in human health, including the eradication of polio. I learned so much from this book about what took place on the campus of Tuskegee Institute (now University); the influence Tuskegee had in medical advancements still thriving today; and how grace played a major role in bringing brilliant minds of both races together for the common good that would benefit all races. As I began to think about what it means to "raise up the man farthest down," the thought occurred to me that the answer lies within each one of us.

Dana Chandler and Edith Powell tell the story of Tuskegee and how the advancements in health care that took place at Tuskegee faced an uphill battle in regard to being accepted by the medical community in White America. In some cases, the advancements made in the laboratories at Tuskegee had to be disguised because they came from a Black institution. "To raise up the man farthest down" in this case meant to raise the White man's veil of ignorance. White America had to be educated that these men and women of Tuskegee, along with other people of color, were not only brilliant, but in many cases were and are smarter and brighter than the best of the White race. This was a major hurdle for both races, but especially the Black race in a place and time where such opportunities were limited.

> People of color were not only brilliant, but in many cases were and are smarter and brighter than the best of the White race.

Then there was the issue of oppression. Arrogantly prejudiced and ignorant White people were simply not going to allow a person of color the merit-based opportunities they had earned. The good news is there always seemed to be a high-minded White doctor or nurse who could see the inherent intellect and knew better, never allowing the color barrier to deny deserved opportunity. These brilliant Black researchers lived with an expectation of being denied, but they were patiently persistent, influencing open minds to accept new discoveries made by "the man farthest down."

As I continued to discover how White people did everything in their power to keep men and women of the Black race down by denying opportunities for them to be raised up, I had more questions. How could this be? How could seemingly civilized human beings, so-called Christians, be so mean-spirited and hateful to other humans created in the image of the same God who created us all? Jesus may have been on their lips in church on Sunday, but He was nonexistent in their hearts the rest of the week. The prophet Jeremiah referred to such hypocrisy when he wrote, "You are near in their mouth but far from their mind" (Jeremiah 12:2).

As I think of the oppression and injustices that were allowed and, in many ways, continue today, I shake my head in disbelief and can only come up with one explanation for this kind of uncivilized and evil behavior toward another image-bearer of God: Jesus Christ was "the man farthest down" in the hearts of White America, and the enemy of God was being exalted. It angers me how White Christians treated the sons and daughters of color who were created in the image of God, just like them, just like me, just like you.

> This is the place where grace takes over.

The apostle John quoted Jesus in his Gospel: "And I, if I am lifted up from the earth, will draw all peoples to Myself" (John 12:32). When Jesus said "all people," He meant *all* people: Red, Yellow, Black, Brown, and White. We are all precious in His sight, and the only way we will ever be at rest with each other is to get out of the way and make room in our hearts for Jesus to rise up. When we do that, He will provide exactly what is needed to bring us together. This is the place where grace outshines race.

It is a battle that continues today in the hearts of all of us. The light that shined in Booker was indeed the Light of the world. To keep that Light shining in us is to allow the Morning Star to rise and shine in our hearts.

> *But thanks be to God that, though you used to be slaves to sin,*
> *you have come to obey from your heart the pattern of teaching*
> *that has now claimed your allegiance. You have been set free from sin*
> *and have become slaves of righteousness.*
> —Romans 6:17-18 (NIV)

Booker was a slave of man's sin who was set free to become a slave of the righteousness of God. His ideology was grounded in a biblical worldview, faith, and grace. God gave Booker His vision for peace on earth, and Booker answered the call at Tuskegee. In spite of being dismissed by the arrogance of both races, Booker showed us how to build a life from the bottom, a hand up versus a handout. He was a servant to God first, then to his fellow man of all races. Booker displayed the Spirit of God in his life, his work, and his love for all people, the same Spirit that became the "Tuskegee spirit." Booker T. Washington lived the process of ascending from a slave of man to a slave of righteousness, under new ownership and new authority.

Do you not know that to whom you present yourselves slaves to obey, you are that one's slaves whom you obey, whether of sin leading to death, or of obedience leading to righteousness? . . . But now having been set free from sin, and having become slaves of God, you have your fruit to holiness, and the end, everlasting life.
—Romans 6:16, 22

Friction from Within

As loved and revered as Dr. Washington was, there were those who opposed his patient and deliberate philosophy and methods of advancing his race. He was opposed by intellectuals of his own race, who considered themselves above Booker's ideology of cooperating with anyone with White skin, for any reason. These elites were educated in the North and possessed classroom knowledge but little walking-around sense. The following passage is a bit long, but it is essential to understand the challenges Washington faced within his own race.

> It makes a great deal of difference in the life of a race, as it does in the life of an individual, whether the world expects much or little of that individual or of that race. I suppose that every boy and every girl born in poverty have felt at some time in their lives the weight of the world against them. What

the people in the communities did not expect them to do it was hard for them to convince themselves that they could do. . . .

The trouble in my case . . . was that the stories we read in school were all concerned with the success and achievements of white boys and men. Occasionally I spoke to some of my schoolmates in regard to the characters of whom I had read, but they invariably reminded me that the stories I had been reading had to do with the members of another race. Sometimes I tried to argue the matter with them, saying that what others had done some of us might also be able to do, and that the lack of a past in our race was no reason why it should not have a future.

> My experience is that people who call themselves "The Intellectuals" understand theories, but they do not understand things.

They replied that our case was entirely different. They said, in effect, that because of our colour and because we carried in our faces the brand of a race that had been in slavery, white people did not want us to succeed.

In the end I usually wound up the discussion by recalling the life of Frederick Douglass, reminding them of the high position which he had reached and of the great service which he had performed for his own race and for the cause of human freedom in the long anti-slavery struggle. . . .

After I became a student at Hampton, under Gen. Samuel C. Armstrong, I heard a great deal more about Frederick Douglass, and I followed all his movements with intense interest. . . .

Some three or four years after I had organized the Tuskegee Institute I invited Mr. Douglass to make a visit to the school and to speak at the commencement exercises of the school. He came and spoke to a great audience, many of whom had driven thirty or forty miles to hear the great orator and leader of the race. . . .

Mr. Douglass's great life-work had been in the political agitation that led to the destruction of slavery. He had been the great defender of the race, and in the struggle to win from Congress and from the country at large the recognition of the Negro's rights as a man and a citizen he had played an important part. But the long and bitter political struggle in which he had engaged against slavery had not prepared Mr. Douglass to take up the equally difficult task of fitting the Negro for the opportunities and responsibilities of freedom. . . .

There has been a small number of white people and an equally small number of coloured people who felt, after my Atlanta speech, that I ought to branch out and discuss political questions, putting emphasis upon the importance of political activity and success for the members of my race. Others, who thought it quite natural that, while I was in the South, I should not say anything that would be offensive, expected that I would cut loose in the North and denounce the Southern people in a way to keep alive and intensify the sectional differences which had sprung up as a result of slavery and the Civil War. Still others thought that there was something lacking in my style of defending the Negro. I went too much into the facts and did not say enough about the Rights of Man and the Declaration of Independence.

When these people found that I did not change my policy as a result of my Atlanta speech, but stuck to my old line of argument, urging the importance of education of the hand, the head, and the heart, they were thoroughly disappointed. So far as my addresses made it appears that the race troubles in the South could be solved by education rather than by political measures, they felt that I was putting the emphasis in the wrong place.

My determination to stand by the programme which I had worked out during the years that I had been at Tuskegee and which I had expressed in my Atlanta speech, soon brought me into conflict with a small group of coloured people who sometimes styled themselves "The Intellectuals," at other times "The Talented Tenth." As most of these men were graduates of Northern colleges and made their homes for the most part in the North, it was natural enough, I suppose, that they should feel that leadership in all race matters should remain, as heretofore, in the North. At any rate, they were opposed to any change from the policy of uncompromising and relentless antagonism to the South so long as there seemed to them to be anything in Southern conditions wrong or unjust to the Negro. . . .

According to their way of looking at the matter, the Southern white man was the natural enemy of the Negro, and any attempt, no matter for what purpose, to gain his sympathy or support must be regarded as a kind of treason to the race. . . .

My experience is that people who call themselves "The Intellectuals" understand theories, but they do not understand things. . . .

For them there was nothing to do but insist on

the application of the abstract principles of protest
. . . . "The Intellectuals" found that the Southern
people rarely, if ever, heard of their protests and, if
they did hear of them, paid no attention to them,
they began to attack the persons nearer home. . . .
They made me a frequent and favourite object of
attack—not merely for the reasons which I have
already stated, but because they felt that if they
attacked me in some particular violent way it would
surprise people and attract attention. . . .

The most surprising thing about this distur-
bance, I confess, is the fact that it was organized
by the very people who have been loudest in condemning the Southern white people because they
had suppressed the expression of opinion on public questions and denied the Negro the right of
free speech. . . .

I do not wish to give the impression by what
I have said that, behind all the intemperance and
extravagance of these men, there is not a vein of
genuine feeling and even at times of something like
real heroism. The trouble is that all this fervour
and intensity is wasted on side issues and trivial
matters. It does not connect itself with anything
that is helpful and constructive. These crusaders, as
nearly as I can see, are fighting windmills.

The truth is, I suspect, as I have already
suggested, that "The Intellectuals" live too much in
the past. They know books but they do not know
men. They know a great deal about the slavery
controversy, for example, but they know almost
nothing about the Negro. Especially are they
ignorant in regard to the actual needs of the masses
of the coloured people in the South to-day. . . .

It is pretty hard, however, to help a young man

who has started wrong. Once he gets the idea that—because he has crammed his head full with mere book knowledge—the world owes him a living, it is hard for him to change. . . .

They have gained the idea at some point in their career that, because they are Negroes, they are entitled to the special sympathy of the world, and they have thus got into the habit of relying on this sympathy rather than on their own efforts to make their way. . . .

Among the most trying class of people with whom I come in contact are the persons who have been educated in books to the extent that they are able, upon every occasion, to quote a phrase or a sentiment from Shakespeare, Milton, Cicero, or some other great writer. Every time any problem arises they are on the spot with a phrase or a quotation. No problem is so difficult that they are not able, with a definition or abstraction of some kind, to solve it. I like phrases, and I frequently find them useful and convenient in conversation, but I have not found in them a solution for many of the actual problems of life.

In college they studied problems and solved them on paper. . . .

Perhaps I ought to add, in order that my statements may not be misleading, that I do not mean to say that the type of college man that I have described is confined to the members of my own race. Every kind of life produces its own peculiar kind of failures, and they are not confined to one race. . . .

There is another class of coloured people who make a business of keeping the troubles, the wrongs, and the hardships of the Negro race before the public. Having learned that they are able to make a living out of their troubles, they have grown into the settled habit of advertising their wrongs—partly because they want sympathy and partly because it pays. Some of these people do not want the Negro to lose his grievances, because they do not want to lose their jobs. . . .

I am afraid that there is a certain class of race-problem solvers who don't want the patient to get well, because as long as the disease holds out they have not only an easy means of making a living, but also an easy medium through which to make themselves prominent before the public. . . .

I confess that all these criticisms and suggestions were not without effect upon my mind. But, after thinking the matter all over, I decided that, pleasant as it might be to follow the programme that was laid out for me, I should be compelled to stick to my original job and work out my salvation along the lines that I had originally laid down for myself. . . .

There are some things that one individual can do for another, and there are some things that one race can do for another. But, on the whole, every individual and every race must work out its own salvation. Let me add that if one thing more than another has taught me to have confidence in the masses of my own people it has been their willingness (and even eagerness) to learn and their disposition to help themselves and depend upon themselves as soon as they have learned how to do so. . . .

I have found in my dealings with the Negro race—and I believe that the same is true of all races that the only way to hold people together is by means of a constructive, progressive programme. It is not argument, nor criticism, nor hatred, but work in constructive effort, that gets hold of men and binds them together in a way to make them rally to the support of a common cause.[14]

As much as Dr. Washington's words illustrate the opposition he faced, they also remind us of the opposition all good men face when confronting pride, complacency, apathy, and even outright evil. The Bible is full of similar challenges, and our Bible heroes are like Washington, those who refused to back down. A passage from the prophet Jeremiah sums it up well: "But they did not obey nor incline their ear, but made their neck stiff, that they might not hear nor receive instruction" (Jeremiah 17:23).

> The lack of a race in our past was no reason why it should not have a future.

Every one of us, regardless of race, must be willing to embrace what is true about us, especially the truth of what God says about each of us. God does not divide us by color or ethnicity, and neither should we. It is God who determines who we are, and it is our responsibility to interpret our unique identity in Christ under His divine guidance for ourselves as well as how we relate to each other.

Booker faced strong opposition, even from the Black community. Friction within the Black community continues to be alive and well today. Polarization among Blacks is at an all-time high, and it boils down to what is in the heart under that beautiful Black skin. The source of the friction has not changed since the days when Dr. Washington faced opposition from W. E. B. Du Bois. The agenda of Du Bois and his so-called "Talented Tenth" was to divide and agitate rather than make any effort to influence the two races to work together.

Later in "Character Grace," you will read one of Dr. Washington's Sunday evening messages on the two sides of life: the bright side and the dark side. On the bright side, you have those whose values are more in line with biblical truth, those more interested in serving. On the dark side is the group who wants nothing to do with the ways of God, demanding that they be served. One side wants to make it a racial issue when it has nothing to do with skin color; it has everything to do with what you believe about God. One side chooses to live victoriously while the other side chooses to blame others for their place in life and remain the victim. One side asks, "Who can I serve?" The other side asks, "How can I be served?" One side gives freedom of choice; the other demands you agree with them. One side calls for justice according to God; the other side demands their rights according to man. W. E. B. Du Bois was the voice of the dark side and, in what is true to our nature, his people, for the most part, chose to believe the lies he spoke about Booker T. Washington that followed the narrative that still pervades the Black race today.

> God does not divide us by color, and neither should we.

It is time for us to return to the ideology of Booker T. Washington. We can do it, but we cannot do it alone. There is no hope for us if we remain divided, not caring to know each other, doing our own thing within the boundaries of those who look like us. I am speaking to everyone here, regardless of the color of your skin. We must come together. It is only when we come together that God will reveal His utmost grace.

> *Behold, how good and how pleasant it is*
> *for brethren to dwell together in unity!*
> —Psalm 133:1

Booker T. Washington's "larger education" reflected an educational system "based on real-world solutions" and "usefulness in the community."[15] He was a man of action while W. E. B Du Bois was a man of rhetoric, always talking without action. He merely talked about and led his people to a life of protest versus progress. Like Washington, Du Bois was educated, but he used his education to divide the races rather than unite them. Booker believed in a world where Blacks and Whites worked together. He knew that whatever we accomplished with our hands, if our hearts were in it, the battle in our minds would be won by our common good. The battle rages on today as it did in 1900. The dark side remains loud and hostile to the loving-kindness of God. The bright side remains steadfast and loyal to the moral authority of God. We all have a choice. We can choose to live abundantly on the bright side, or we can choose to live in misery on the dark side. It ain't rocket science. We've followed the dark side of division long enough. Let there be light.

> *"Associate yourself with people of good quality,*
> *for it is better to be alone than to be in bad company."*
> —Booker T. Washington

CHAPTER THREE

The Power of Influence

I happen to know men to whom I am indebted for many things,
but most of all for what they have done for me in teaching
me to value all men at their real worth regardless of race or colour.
—Booker T. Washington

We all have influences in our lives. Who we listen to, who we hang out with, what we read—they all influence what we believe about God, ourselves, and who we will become. Booker T. Washington was no different, but he did something most of us rarely think about, let alone take the time to do. He wrote about the men and women of influence in his life. Booker was an observer of men and women, and he interpreted people. He was never in the company of a man that he didn't learn something from. He was intentional to learn something that would add to his character or something he wanted no part of. Author Andy Andrews wrote the novel *The Noticer*. Booker T. Washington was a noticer.

> **One thing they all have in common is they were authentic in character.**

In this chapter, we will take a look at many of the men and women—of both the Black and the White race—who influenced Booker T. Washington. It is revealing and heartwarming how he described those who most influenced his character development. Some are Black and some are White, but one thing they all have in common is they were authentic in character. Booker cared less about the color of a person's skin and more about what was under it, in the heart, and who the man or woman was. The people in this chapter are listed in chronological order, from his early life until his final days on planet Earth. The words are Washington's, according to his writings in *Up from Slavery* and *My Larger Education*.

Jane Ferguson, Booker T. Washington's Mother:

> There was not a single member of my race anywhere near us who could read, and I was too timid to approach any of the white people. . . . In all my efforts to learn to read my mother shared full my ambition, and sympathized with me and aided me in every way that she could. Though she was totally ignorant, so far as mere book knowledge was concerned, she had high ambitions for her children, and a large fund of good hard, common sense which seemed to enable her to meet and master every situation. If I have done anything in life worth attention, I feel sure that I inherited the disposition from my mother.[1]

Mrs. Viola Ruffner, Wife of General Lewis Ruffner, owner of the salt furnace and coal mine where Booker T. Washington worked as a boy:

> I was on fire constantly with one ambition, and that was to go to Hampton. . . .
>
> After hearing of the Hampton Institute, I continued to work for a few months longer in the coal-mine. While at work there, I heard of a vacant position in the household of General Lewis Ruffner,

the owner of the salt-furnace and coal-mine. Mrs. Viola Ruffner, the wife of General Ruffner, was a "Yankee" woman from Vermont. Mrs. Ruffner had a reputation all through the vicinity for being very strict with her servants, and especially with the boys who tried to serve her. Few of them had remained with her more than two or three weeks. They all left with the same excuse: she was too strict. I decided, however, that I would rather try Mrs. Ruffner's house than remain in the coal-mine, and so my mother applied to her for the vacant position. I was hired at a salary of $5 per month.

I had heard so much about Mrs. Ruffner's severity that I was almost afraid to see her, and trembled when I went into her presence. I had not lived with her many weeks, however, before I began to understand her. . . .

I cannot now recall how long I lived with Mrs. Ruffner before going to Hampton, but I think it must have been a year and a half. At any rate, I here repeat what I have said more than once before, that the lessons that I learned in the home of Mrs. Ruffner were as valuable to me as any education I have ever gotten anywhere since. . . .

From fearing Mrs. Ruffner I soon learned to look upon her as one of my best friends. When she found that she could trust me she did so implicitly. . . . It was while living with her that I began to get together my first library. I secured a dry-goods box, knocked out one side of it, put some shelves in it, and began putting into it every kind of book that I could get my hands upon, and called it my "library."[2]

Miss Nathalie Lord, Teacher of Booker T. Washington:

> Perhaps the most valuable thing that I got out of my
> second year [at Hampton] was an understanding of
> the use and value of the Bible. Miss Nathalie Lord,
> one of the teachers, from Portland, Maine, taught
> me how to use and love the Bible. Before this I had
> never cared a great deal about it, but now I learned
> to love to read the Bible, not only for the spiritual
> help which it gives, but on account of it as literature.
> The lessons taught me in this respect took such a
> hold upon me that at the present time, when I am
> at home, no matter how busy I am, I always make it
> a rule to read a chapter or a portion of a chapter in
> the morning, before beginning the work of the day.
>   Whatever ability I may have as a public speaker
> I owe in a measure to Miss Lord. When she found
> out that I had some inclination in this direction, she
> gave me private lessons in the matter of breathing,
> emphasis, and articulation.[3]

General Samuel Armstrong, Civil War General and Founder
of a school for African and Native Americans that later became
Hampton Institute in Virginia:

> I have spoken of the impression that was made
> upon me by the buildings and general appearance
> of the Hampton Institute, but I have not spoken
> of that which made the greatest and most lasting
> impression upon me, and that was a great man—
> the noblest, rarest human being that it has ever
> been my privilege to meet. I refer to the late General
> Samuel C. Armstrong.
>   It has been my fortune to meet personally many

of what are called great characters, both in Europe and America, but I do not hesitate to say that I never met any man who, in my estimation, was the equal of General Armstrong. Fresh from the degrading influences of the slave plantation and the coal-mines, it was a rare privilege for me to be permitted to come into direct contact with such a character as General Armstrong. I shall always remember that the first time I went into his presence he made the impression upon me of being a perfect man: I was made to feel that there was something about him that was superhuman. It was my privilege to know the General personally from the time I entered Hampton till he died, and the more I saw of him the greater he grew in my estimation. One might have removed from Hampton all the buildings, classrooms, teachers, and industries, and given the men and women there the opportunity of coming into daily contact with General Armstrong, and that alone would have been a liberal education. The older I grow, the more I am convinced that there is no education which one can get from [books] and costly apparatus that is equal to that which can be gotten from contact with great men and women. Instead of studying books so constantly, how I wish that our schools and colleges might learn to study men and things! . . .

Although he fought the Southern white man in the Civil War, I never heard him utter a bitter word against him afterward. On the other hand, he was constantly seeking to find ways by which he could be of service to the Southern whites. . . .

I have spoken of my admiration for General Armstrong, and yet he was but a type of that

Christlike body of men and women who went into the Negro schools at the close of the war by the hundreds to assist in lifting up my race. The history [of] the world fails to show a higher, purer, and more unselfish class of men and women than those who found their way into those Negro schools. . . .

General Armstrong spent two of the last six months of his life in my home at Tuskegee. At that time he was paralyzed to the extent that he had lost control of his body and voice in a very large degree. Notwithstanding his affliction, he worked almost constantly night and day for the cause to which he had given his life. I never saw a man who so completely lost sight of himself. I do not believe he ever had a selfish thought. He was just as happy in trying to assist some other institution in the South as he was when working for Hampton.[4]

Lewis Adams and George Campbell, Former Slave and Former Slave Owner who wrote to General Armstrong in search of a teacher for a school to educate Blacks and poor Whites in Alabama. On General Armstrong's recommendation, Adams and Campbell hired Booker T. Washington and became board members when the school became Tuskegee Institute:

In the midst of all the difficulties which I encountered in getting the little school started, and since then through a period of nineteen years, there are two men among all the many friends of the school in Tuskegee upon whom I have depended constantly for advice and guidance; and the success of the undertaking is largely due to these men, from whom I have never sought anything in vain. I mentioned them simply as types. One is a

white man and an ex-slaveholder, Mr. George W.
Campbell; the other is a black man and an ex-slave,
Mr. Lewis Adams. These were the men who wrote
to General Armstrong for a teacher. . . .

I do not know two men, one an ex-slaveholder,
one an ex-slave, whose advice and judgment I
would feel more like following in everything which
concerns the life and development of the school at
Tuskegee than those of these two men.[5]

Theodore Roosevelt, U.S. President and Friend of Booker T.
Washington:

I was thrown, comparatively early in my career, in
contact with Colonel Roosevelt. He was just the
sort of man to whom any one who was trying to do
work of any kind for the improvement of any race
or type of humanity would naturally go to for advice
and help. I have seen him and been in close contact
with him under many varying circumstances and
I confess that I have learned much from studying
his career, both while he was in office and since he
has been in private life. One thing that impresses
me about Mr. Roosevelt is that I have never known
him, having given a promise, to overlook or forget
it; in fact, he seems to forget nothing, not even the
most trivial incidents. I found him the same when
he was President that he was as a private citizen, or
as Governor of New York, or as Vice President of
the United States. In fact, I have no hesitation in
saying that I consider him the highest type of all-
round man that I have ever met. . . .

In the case of the average man, it has seemed to
me that as soon as he gets into office he becomes

an entirely different man. Some men change for the better under the weight of responsibility; others change for the worse. I never could understand what there is in American politics that so fatally alters the character of a man. . . .

Of course, not all men who go into politics are affected in the way that I have described. Let me add that I have known many public men and have studied them carefully, but the best and highest example of a man that was the same in political office that he was in private life is Col. Theodore Roosevelt. . . .

During President Roosevelt's administration I was asked to go as a Commissioner of the United States to Liberia. . . .

Mr. Roosevelt appointed other coloured men to high office in the North and West, but I think that any one who examines into the individual qualifications of the coloured men appointed to office by Mr. Roosevelt will find, in each case, that they were what he insisted that they should be— men of superior ability and of superior character.

President Taft happily has followed the same policy. . . .

Mr. Roosevelt and Mr. Taft have had another purpose in appointing to office the kind of coloured people that I have named. They have said that they desire the persons appointed by them to be men of the highest character in order that the younger generation of coloured people might see that men of conspicuous ability and conspicuous purity of character are recognized in politics as in other walks of life. They have hoped that such recognition might lead other coloured people to strive to attain a high reputation.

Mr. Roosevelt did not apply this rule to the appointments of coloured people alone. He believed that he could . . . change the tone of politics in the South and improve the relations of the races by the appointment of men who stood high in their professions and who were not only friendly to the coloured people but had the confidence of the white people as well.[6]

Booker T. and Teddy had vision. They had drive. And their skins were tough enough that they drove forward even in the face of often vicious criticism. We are a better nation because they chose to fight; they would not settle, recognizing that progress is always a battle.
—Brian Kilmeade, *Teddy and Booker T.*

CHAPTER FOUR

Friends in High Places

*Booker Washington is to rank with the few immortals
as one who has not only shown his people the promised land,
but is teaching them to prove themselves worthy of it—
a Joshua and Moses combined.*
—Andrew Carnegie

Booker T. Washington was never attracted to politics or to Washington, D.C. Nor was he particularly comfortable while visiting our nation's capital. It was troubling to him what he observed in those who went to Washington. He was

concerned about the changes in their character from the dark influences that pervaded in our nation's capital in those days, and as far as I can tell, nothing has changed. He thought many of those of his race who chose to live in D.C. did so for the perceived and immediate rise in status. He was more concerned with a person's character than their status in the political arena. He wrote,

> I do not think that I ever shared that feeling of so many others of my race. I never liked the atmosphere of Washington. I early saw that it was impossible to build up a race of which the leaders were spending most of their time, thought, and energy in trying to get into office, or in trying to stay there after they were in. So, for the greater part of my life, I have avoided Washington; and even now I rarely spend a day in that city which I do not look upon as a day of practically thrown away. . . .
>
> In the case of the average man, it has seemed to me that as soon as he gets into office he becomes an entirely different man. Some men change for the better under the weight of responsibility; others change for the worse. I never could understand what there is in American politics that so fatally alters the character of a man. I have known men, who, in their private life and in their business, were scrupulously careful to keep their word—men who would never, directly or indirectly, deceive any one with whom they were associated. When they took political office all this changed. . . .
>
> This sort of change that comes over people after they get [into] office is not confined, however, to the Negro race. Other races seem to suffer in the same way. . . .

Because of these facts, as well as for other reasons, I have never sought nor accepted a political position.[1]

While understanding the risks and challenges of politics, particularly at the national level, Dr. Washington also understood the realities of power and influence. He made an exception to his avoidance of politics when, during President Theodore Roosevelt's administration, he was asked to serve as Commissioner of the United States to Liberia. He was a close friend to President Roosevelt and did not want to disappoint. In his words:

> In considering whether I should accept this position, it was urged that, because of the work that I had already done in this country for my own people and because my name was already known to some extent to the people of Liberia, I was the person best fitted to undertake the work that the Government wanted done. While I did not like the job and could ill spare the time from the work which I was trying to do for the people of my own race in America, I finally decided to accept the position. I was very happy, however, when President Taft kindly decided to relieve me from the necessity of making the trip and allowed my secretary, Mr. Emmett J. Scott, to go to Africa in my stead. This was as near as I ever came to holding a Government job. But there are other ways of getting into politics than by holding office.[2]

I never could understand what there is in American politics that so fatally alters the character of a man.

Booker always seemed to have his priorities in the right order. While he agreed to serve his country, his loyalty was to make sure his best efforts were spent in representing his race and his responsibilities at Tuskegee. He was cautious in his approach to politics, but he knew his mission to unite people of all races would require at least some participation. As his reputation grew, his ability to fulfill his goals drew him into relationships with prominent and important national and international figures. President Roosevelt became an ally and a friend.

Booker met Colonel Roosevelt early in his career. He was drawn to Roosevelt because the colonel was a good man who was genuinely interested in helping to improve conditions and provide opportunities for any race or for humanity in general. Booker had the opportunity many times to sit and talk with Roosevelt, even after he became president. He said the thing that most impressed him about the president was that he always kept his word, even in trivial matters. According to Booker, Roosevelt had an innate ability not to forget anything, and he was purposeful in every way. Booker shared the fascinating story of their friendship:

> I first became acquainted with Mr. Roosevelt through correspondence. Later, in one of my talks with him—and this was a time when there seemed little chance of his ever becoming President. . . . He spoke out, as is his custom, that which was in his mind. Even then, many years before he attained his ambition, he began to outline to me how he wanted to help not only the Negro, but the whole South, should he ever become President. I question whether any man ever went into the Presidency with a more sincere desire to be of real service to the South than Mr. Roosevelt did. . . .
>
> Practically everything that he tried to do for the South while he was President was outlined in

conversations to me many years before it became known to most people that he had the slightest chance of becoming President. What he did was not a matter of impulse but the result of carefully matured plans. . . .

Before Mr. Roosevelt became President, not a single coloured man had ever been appointed, so far as I know, to a Federal office in any Northern state. Mr. Roosevelt determined to set the example by placing a coloured man in a high office in his own home city, so that the county might see that he did not want other parts of the country to accept that which he himself was not willing to receive. . . . Mr. Roosevelt appointed other coloured men to high office in the North and West, but I think that any one who examines into the individual qualifications of the coloured men appointed to office by Mr. Roosevelt will find, in each case, that they were what he insisted that they should be— men of superior ability and of superior character.[3]

Dr. Washington was well received in Washington, D.C., New York City, Boston, and many other places of influence. He was friends with many of the Northeast's finest men, including Andrew Carnegie, John D. Rockefeller, and Julius Rosenwald. He was even friends with U.S. Presidents Theodore Roosevelt, Grover Cleveland, William McKinley, Howard Taft, and Woodrow Wilson.

Booker's grace, his heart to serve his fellow man, his commitment to unite the races, his faith, and his relational skills led to him having friends from one end of the social spectrum to the other. He was as at

He was easy to be around and was respected wherever he went.

home with heads of state as he was sitting by the fire in a cabin on a plantation in the South. He was easy to be around and was respected wherever he went. People loved him because they knew he genuinely cared for them and was steadfast and loyal in promoting and protecting their well-being whether they were Black or White.

The following letters illustrate the depth of his relationships. These people were more than acquaintances; they were trusted friends and supporters of him personally and his efforts at Tuskegee. They held Booker in the highest of esteem. These letters are regrets from those who could not attend a luncheon in England, planned to honor of Dr. Washington.

> Dear Mr. Harris:
>
> I regret exceedingly to miss any opportunity of doing honor to one of the greatest men living, Booker Washington. Taking into account his start in life, born a slave, and now the acknowledged leader of his people, I do not know a parallel to the ascent he has made. He has marched steadily upward to undisputed leadership, carrying with this the confidence and approval of the white race, and winning the warm friendship of its foremost members—a double triumph.
>
> Booker Washington is to rank with the few immortals as one who has not only shown his people the promised land, but is teaching them to prove themselves worthy of it—a Joshua and Moses combined.
>
> Very truly yours,
> (Signed) Andrew Carnegie[4]

And:

It is a great disappointment to me that paramount engagements far away from London render it impossible for me to be present at the gathering which is to give greeting and Godspeed to Mr. Booker T. Washington's acquaintance, and I share with all those who know the facts, the appreciation of the services he has rendered and is rendering to the solution of one of the gravest and most perplexing problems of our time. He is a man who, in every sense, deserves well of his contemporaries, and I believe that, when hereafter the story is written of Christian people's endeavor in our day to atone for and to amend the racial wrongdoing of the past, Mr. Booker T. Washington's name will stand in the very forefront of those for whom the world will give thanks.

Archbishop of Canterbury[5]

Regarding his trip to London, Washington said,

I learned in England to see that the race problem in the United States is, as Mr. Herbert Samuels, the English postmaster-general said, "a problem which faces all countries in which races of a widely divergent type are living side by side."

The success of the Negro in America and the progress which had been made here in the solution of the racial problem gained wider and deeper meaning for me as a result of my visit to Europe.[6]

Harvard

Booker T. Washington regarded education as critical to the success of his race. He became educated, shepherded Tuskegee Institute to a reputation of excellence in education, and personally guided countless people to academic achievement. He never attended Harvard but was granted an honorary degree. He described the experience:

> More than once I have been asked what was the greatest surprise that ever came to me. I have little hesitation in answering that question. It was the following letter, which came to me one Sunday morning when I was sitting on the veranda of my home at Tuskegee, surrounded by my wife and three children:
>
> Harvard University
> Cambridge
> May 28, 1896
>
> President Booker T. Washington,
> My Dear Sir: Harvard University desires to confer on you at the approaching Commencement an honorary degree; but it is our custom to confer degrees only on gentlemen who are present. Our Commencement occurs this year on June 24, and your presence would be desirable from about noon till about five o'clock in the afternoon. Would it be possible for you to be in Cambridge on that day?
>
> Believe me, with great regard,
> Very truly yours,
> Charles W. Eliot
>
> This was a recognition that had never in the slightest manner entered into my mind, and it was

hard for me to realize that I was to be honoured by a degree from the oldest and most renowned university in America. As I sat upon my veranda, with this letter in my hand, tears came into my eyes. My whole former life—my life as a slave on the plantation, my work in the coal-mine, the times when I was without food and clothing, when I made my bed under a sidewalk, my struggles for an education, the trying days I had had at Tuskegee, days when I did not know where to turn for a dollar to continue the work there, the ostracism and sometimes oppression of my race—all this passed before me and nearly overcame me. . . .

After these exercises were over, those who had received honorary degrees were invited to lunch with the President. . . .

Among the speakers after dinner were President Eliot, Governor Roger Wolcott, General Miles, Dr. Minot J. Savage, the Hon. Henry Cabot Lodge, and myself. When I was called upon, I said, among other things:

It would in some measure relieve my embarrassment if I could, even in a slight degree, feel myself worthy of the great honour which you do me to-day. Why you have called me from the Black Belt of the South, from among my humble people, to share in the honours of this occasion, is not for me to explain; and yet it may not be inappropriate for me to suggest that it seems to me that one of the most vital questions that touch our American life is how to bring the strong, wealthy, and learned into helpful touch with the poorest, most ignorant, and humblest, and at the same time make one appreciate the vitalizing, strengthening influence of the other. How shall we make the mansions on [yon] Beacon Street feel and see the need of the spirits in the lowliest cabin in Alabama cottonfields or Louisiana sugar-bottoms? This problem Harvard University is solving, not by bringing itself down, but by bringing the masses up.

If my life in the past has meant anything in the lifting up of my people and the bringing about of better relations between your race and mine, I assure you from this day it will mean doubly more. In the economy of God there is but one standard by which an individual can succeed—there is but one for a race. This country demands that every race shall measure itself by the American standard. By it a race must rise or fall, succeed or fail, and in the last analysis mere sentiment counts for little. During the next half-century and more, my race must continue passing through the severe American crucible. We are to be tested in our patience, our forbearance, our perseverance, our power to endure wrong, to withstand temptations, to economize, to acquire and use skill; in our ability to compete, to succeed in commerce, to disregard the superficial for the real, the appearance for the substance, to be great and yet small, learned and yet simple, high and yet the servant of all.

As this was the first time that a New England university had conferred an honorary degree upon a Negro, it was the occasion of much newspaper comment throughout the country. A correspondent of a New York paper said:

When the name Booker T. Washington was called, and he arose to acknowledge and accept, there was such an outburst of applause as greeted not other name except that of the popular soldier, General Miles. The applause was not studied and stiff, sympathetic and condoling; it was enthusiasm and admiration. Every part of the audience from pit to gallery joined in, and a glow covered the cheeks of those around me, proving sincere appreciation of the rising struggle of an ex-slave and the work he has accomplished.

A Boston newspaper said, editorially:

In conferring the honorary degree of Master of Arts upon the Principal of Tuskegee Institute, Harvard University has honoured itself as well as the object of this distinction. The work which Professor Booker T. Washington has accomplished for the education, good citizenship, and popular enlightenment in his chosen field of labour in the South entitles him to rank with our national benefactors. The university which can acclaim him on its list of sons, whether in regular course or honoris causa, may be proud.

It has been mentioned that Mr. Washington is the first of his race to receive an honorary degree from a New England university. This, in itself, is a distinction. But the degree was not conferred because Mr. Washington is a coloured man, or because he was born in slavery, but because he has shown, by his work for the elevation of the people of the Black Belt of the South, a genius and a broad humanity which count for greatness in any man, whether his skin be white or black....

A correspondent of the *New York Times* wrote:

> All the speeches were enthusiastically received, but the coloured man carried off the oratorical honours, and the applause which broke out when he had finished was vociferous and long-continued.[7]

The commitment to excellence in education followed Dr. Washington his entire life. Through his own achievements, and those he led, he left an indelible mark on students, educators, civic leaders, philanthropists, business leaders, political leaders of the highest offices, and, of course, his family and friends. By grace, he established friendships with those still living in the poorest areas, and equally with the most powerful and affluent. He blurred the divisions between the races like none before him. He gave us a template to replicate to restore his successes and reach a level of racial harmony he envisioned and Dr. Martin Luther King Jr. dreamed about.

Like you, I struggle with believing what I want to believe instead of keeping the door of my mind open to the real truth. I have an opinion on just about everything—and too many of those things are just not that important. Most of my opinions are not essential to the main thing, which is to love Jesus and to have a calm spirit toward the opinions of others. In order to keep the main thing the main thing, we must not allow our opinions to fuel any need to be heard. Anytime we feel the need to shout, we are more than likely to be wrong about whatever it is we want to shout about. We must remain civilized toward each other, especially when we have different opinions—which is most of the time. Dr. Washington said, "We can be as separate as the fingers, yet one as the hand."[8] That is a wise statement and one I believe remains as true today as it was when Dr. Washington said it.

*The Tuskegee Idea always asks one question, and that is,
"What are you?" and not, "What have you?"
The man who does not rise superior to his possessions
does not measure up to the Tuskegee idea of manhood.*
—Emmett J. Scott, Tuskegee and Its People

PART II

Education Grace

The Tuskegee idea is that correct education begins at the bottom, and expands naturally as the necessities of the people expand. As the race grows in knowledge, experience, culture, taste, and wealth, its wants are bound to become more and more diverse; and to satisfy these wants there will be gradually developed within our own ranks—as has already been true of the whites—a constantly increasing variety of professional and business men and women.
—Booker T. Washington

CHAPTER FIVE

Tuskegee: Template of Excellence

*In great deeds something abides. On great fields something stays.
Forms change and pass; bodies disappear but spirits linger, to
consecrate ground for the vision-place of souls. And reverent men
and women from afar, and generations that know us not and that
we know not of, heart-drawn to see where and by whom great
things were suffered and done for them, shall come [here] to ponder
and dream; and lo! The shadow of a mighty presence shall wrap
them in its bosom, and the power of the vision pass into their souls.*
—Joshua Lawrence Chamberlain

Hallowed Ground

On July 4, 1881, a tiny hill in Macon County, Alabama, became hallowed ground as the "power of the vision" became reality, and Tuskegee Institute became the Southern center of learning for the Black race and a template of light to a dark world. Tuskegee became a powerful influencer, not just in education but in the progression of industrial training, agriculture, and health care excellence. On this day, Tuskegee Normal School, now known as Tuskegee University, was founded and led by Booker T. Washington.

Together, these two men, one Black and one White, fulfilled a need in the community.

The Tuskegee story began when Lewis Adams, a former slave, and George Campbell, a former slave owner, collaborated on the idea of establishing a school for young Blacks to get an education and grow in every way, including learning how to work with their hands, transform their hearts, and develop minds set on serving the greater good for mankind. Lewis Adams was not just a former slave; he was considered a man of common sense with many skills, which included blacksmithing and gunsmithing. Adams was favored because of the freedoms he experienced from learning to read. He had a White partner, named Lee, and the two men carried on these trades in a store that was more patronized by White people than by people of color. Together, these two men, one Black and one White, fulfilled a need in the community, not just from their retail establishment, but also by showing the community the importance of working together as equals.

Adams had a warm personality, was respected as a man of good judgment, and was influential politically. It was Adams who first mentioned the idea of establishing a state normal school for the purpose of educating Blacks as well as poor Whites.

A bill was passed in the Alabama legislature to appropriate two thousand dollars to be used as salaries in a school for training colored teachers. Students would be admitted free as long as they would agree to become teachers in the public schools once they graduated. The bill was approved by the Negro members of the legislature and passed in the Senate on February 12, 1881. It was approved by the governor, and he appointed George W. Campbell as chairman of the board of three commissioners, one of whom was Lewis Adams.

As a result, these two men joined forces—Adams, the former slave, with Campbell, the former slave owner—and together, they planted the seed that would become Tuskegee Institute. Lewis Adams and George Campbell made a decision that changed the lives of thousands who not only were educated at Tuskegee but were influenced by Booker T. Washington and later George Washington Carver when he came to Tuskegee in 1896.

The freedoms and safe environment within the boundaries of Tuskegee Institute remind me of something Brennan Manning said in his book *All Is Grace*, regarding the sandbox at the playground where he played when he was a boy: "It had definite boundaries but inside those edges I was free to dig and build and to just be."[1]

I am also reminded of how much safer our schools would be if they were designated "Tuskegee Safe," where we secured the perimeter around every school so that boys and girls could play without fear of being attacked from the outside.

The details of Tuskegee are endless. Some of what is presented are dark reminders of our past, but so much of the efficiencies Dr. Washington built into the process certainly still apply today. The beauty in the stories of Tuskegee was of men and women of both races working together. There was a kindred spirit common among them. The color of their skin had no bearing on the effectiveness of the mission. It was an uphill battle, but on top of that tiny hill in Macon County, God did some of His best work in the men and women of Tuskegee.

> **The beauty in the stories of Tuskegee was of men and women of both races working together.**

*The sight of the new building made it a day of
Thanksgiving for them never to be forgotten.*
—Booker T. Washington

In the fall of 1882, Dr. Washington took a trip north to secure funds for a new building on the campus of Tuskegee. The first place he went was Northampton, Massachusetts. Following are Dr. Washington's words regarding the funds he acquired for the construction of Porter Hall and the first Thanksgiving at Tuskegee.

> We were successful in getting money enough so
> that on Thanksgiving Day of that year we held our

first service in the chapel of Porter Hall, although the building was not completed.

In looking about for some one to preach the Thanksgiving sermon, 1 found one of the rarest men that it has ever been my privilege to know. This was the Rev. Robert C. Bedford, a white man from Wisconsin, who was then pastor of a little coloured Congregational church in Montgomery, Ala. Before going to Montgomery to look for some one to preach this sermon 1 had never heard of Mr. Bedford. He had never heard of me. He gladly consented to come to Tuskegee and hold the Thanksgiving service. It was the first service of the kind that the colored people there had ever observed, and what a deep interest they manifested in it! The sight of the new building made it a day of Thanksgiving for them never to be forgotten.

Mr. Bedford consented to become one of the trustees of the school, and in that capacity, and as a worker for it, he has been connected with it for eighteen years. During this time he has borne the school upon his heart night and day, and is never so happy as when he is performing some service, no matter how humble, for it. He completely obliterates himself in everything, and looks only for permission to serve where service is most disagreeable, and where others would not be attracted. In all my relations with him he has seemed to me to approach as nearly to the spirit of the Master as almost any man 1 ever met.[2]

The hallowed ground of Tuskegee Normal School became the manifestation of what had been growing inside Booker T. Washington's mind all of his life. What he learned from his childhood days in slavery, from General Armstrong at Hampton, from his experience with the Native American boys, from the influential men and women throughout his life, and by the grace of God converged at Tuskegee. Tuskegee was the outward expression of what had been growing in the heart of Washington his entire life. He was tireless in his pursuit of excellence inside the boundaries of the Institute, but more so the character inside the students and teachers.

Dr. Washington was as practical as he was philosophical. He faced his problems head-on and refused to back down. He applied grace and wisdom to carve a better path for those he was leading. Tuskegee Institute faced many challenges, but through his strong leadership, he was able to guide the board, faculty, staff, and students down a path of excellence. Tuskegee was self-sufficient. There was no other choice because of the hostility outside the boundaries of the Institute. One great example of the independence that thrived under the leadership of Washington was the idea of making bricks. Making bricks filled a need in Macon and the surrounding southeast Alabama area and also created a sense of appreciation in Whites for these capable men and women of the Black race.

> From the very beginning, at Tuskegee, I was determined to have the students do not only the agricultural and domestic work, but to have them erect their own buildings. My plan was to have them, while performing this service, taught the latest and best methods of labour, so that the school would not only get the benefit of their efforts, but the students themselves would be taught to see not only utility in labour, but beauty and dignity; would be taught, in fact, how to lift labour up from mere drudgery and toil, and would learn to love work for its own sake. . . .
>
> In the early days of the school, I think my most

trying experience was in the matter of brickmaking. As soon as we got the farm work reasonably well started, we directed our next efforts toward the industry of making bricks. We needed these for use in connection with the erection of our own buildings; but there was also another reason for establishing this industry. There was no brickyard in the town, and in addition to our own needs there was a demand for bricks in the general market. . . .

The making of these bricks taught me an important lesson in regard to the relations of the two races in the South. Many white people who had had no contact with the school, and perhaps no sympathy with it, came to us to buy bricks because they found out that ours were good bricks. They discovered that we were supplying a real want in the community. The making of these bricks caused many of the white residents of the neighbourhood to begin to feel that the education of the Negro was not making him worthless, but that in educating our students we were adding something to the wealth and comfort of the community. As the people of the neighbourhood came to us to buy bricks, we got acquainted with them; they traded with us and we with them. Our business interests became intermingled. We had something which they wanted; they had something which we wanted. This, in a large measure, helped to lay the foundation for the pleasant relations that have continued to exist between us and the white people in that section, and which now extend throughout the South.

Wherever one of our brickmakers has gone in the South, we find that he has something to contribute to the well-being of the community into which he has gone; something that has made the community feel that, in a degree, it is indebted to him, and perhaps, to a certain extent, dependent upon him. In this way pleasant relations between the races have been stimulated.

My experience is that there is something in human nature which always makes an individual recognize and reward merit, no matter under what colour of skin merit is found. I have found, too, that it is the visible, the tangible, that goes a long ways in softening prejudices.[3]

> *The individual who can do something*
> *the world wants done will, in the end,*
> *make his way regardless of his race.*
> —Booker T. Washington

Chosen by God

Tuskegee was chosen by God as a place to manifest His gracious idea of heaven on earth, a promised land, and a proving ground for America to follow. God put His absolute best in Booker T. Washington, raising him up from the lowest of lows and, by His grace, demonstrating His highest and best for mankind. The character of Christ abided in Booker T. Washington. He made the most of every opportunity that came his way. God gave us an image of what grace truly is in the Tuskegee story. Grace is God's presence on His creation in even the most unlikely situations—a slave being humble in spirit as he navigated an unlikely ascent to the top. Dr. Washington had something men and women, even presidents, desired. His success is measured in the influence he had on the many and by the obstacles he overcame in his journey to unprecedented prominence. Booker T. Washington lived a life worth imitating.

You read about several men and women who influenced the life of Booker T. Washington in chapter 3. Perhaps the one who had the greatest influence on him was his mother. The influence Washington's mom had on him lives on in his influence on mankind, and specifically on me. What I have written about a man I never knew, a man whom I have grown to love, is overflowing with heartfelt gratitude and utmost respect. I am unworthy and woefully inadequate of doing justice to this great American, incapable of giving him his due in expressing his profound influence on me and how much more at peace our culture would be had we adopted and practiced his teachings and methods. There is a deep and newly discovered reverence for the life of a man whom God spoke through at Tuskegee—and his words continue to speak to the masses of all nations today. As I read the following Scripture passage, I immediately thought of Booker T. Washington. He battled injustices yet represented his people well and always spoke graciously of White people.

> For though we walk in the flesh, we do not war according to the flesh. For the weapons of our warfare are not carnal but mighty in God for pulling down strongholds, casting down arguments and every high thing that exalts itself against the knowledge of God, bringing every thought into captivity to the obedience of Christ. (2 Corinthians 10:3-5)

In all the knowledge I have gathered regarding Booker T. Washington, I find absolutely no evidence that he ever exalted himself. Whether in his autobiography, in his Sunday chapel messages to the students and faculty at Tuskegee, to U.S. presidents and world leaders, or on the world stage, the words he spoke were seasoned with grace. He had a humble willingness to express the love and grace of God and to magnify his Maker in serving others, making the world better. He personified the fruit of the Spirit as the apostle Paul described in Galatians: "But the fruit of the Spirit is love, joy, peace, longsuffering, kindness, goodness, faithfulness, gentleness, self-control" (Galatians 5:22-23).

Washington didn't fight his battles from an elevated spirit of pride, haughtiness, or agitation. He fought on his knees, and his view of life was always from the bottom, serving his fellow man. Even for those he knew opposed him and the Black race, he never allowed himself to harbor any bitterness toward them. He often described the measure of a man as what is under skin. Appearances were meaningless to Washington. It was all about what was real and lasting.

Appearances were meaningless to Washington. It was all about what was real and lasting.

In reading the resurrected story of Tuskegee, I hope we have found a hidden treasure, a pearl of wisdom, something that draws us to the character and teachings of Booker T. Washington. Hopefully, we have discovered that the Tuskegee template remains relevant today.

It is up to you and me whether we live according to the divided status quo or choose to make a difference by entering the divide, not thinking less of ourselves but thinking of ourselves less. It is in the divide we will find grace, and when we find grace, grace will find us. God created us for community—first with Him, then with each other. While all people are different on the outside, it is by God's amazing grace that we allow others to peek into the very soul of our heart and discover that we are indeed equal.

He should be regarded as "America's Greatest Teacher."

The apostle Paul wrote in 1 Corinthians, "Imitate me, just as I also imitate Christ" (1 Corinthians 11:1). We are all imitators of someone. Dr. Washington is the kind of man we should all choose to imitate if we are serious about the most important things in life. Building character begins in the home, and we could not make a better choice for the teacher in our homes than this man who, in my opinion, most imitated Christ. Dr. Washington lived and loved as Jesus Christ did. He should be regarded as "America's Greatest Teacher." We would be a more loving country today had we heeded his call and followed his lead, under the authority of God, for the last one hundred and fifty years. There is no greater role model to whom you can introduce to your children.

Today, we are living the legacy we will leave our families and the world around us. We choose whether that legacy is one of rest or unrest, peace or war, unity or division, kindness or agitation. We all see the legacy Dr. Washington left at Tuskegee and how he did his best to influence the world for the common good. We can do likewise, if we so choose.

We have more than enough evidence that the choices our people made, both Black and White, over the past one hundred years have not led to unity. What I have learned from perhaps the most brilliant man of any race, other than Christ, has transformed my heart in countless ways. We choose where we cast down our bucket every day, in every moment. Please join me in casting down your bucket among the peacemakers in the living waters of Jesus Christ. He is "the way, the truth, and the life" (John 14:6). Let's celebrate Tuskegee and the spirit of unity together. The choice is yours. It's your call.

> *You and I just don't have the choice of opting out.*
> *We are relational beings who have been called to lifelong*
> *community with God and others.*
> —Paul David Tripp

Education That Educates

Dr. Washington believed in education for all people. He was a believer in the education one receives from books, but he also believed in the education from experiences in life. In the fall of 1898, President McKinley and his cabinet visited Tuskegee Institute. The preparation for the event, along with the fanfare, was somewhat disruptive to the classroom routine, and some of the students failed to see the value of investing time in such events. Washington rarely, if ever, missed an opportunity to teach beyond the obvious, helping students see the value of learning outside the classroom, in organizing and effectively executing such events:

> When interruptions come such as we have just had, taking you away from your regular routine work and study, and the preparation of routine lessons is interrupted, the first thought to some may be that this time is lost, in so far as it relates to education

in the ordinary sense; that it is so much time taken away from that part of one's life that should be devoted to acquiring education. I suppose that during the last few days the questions have come to many of you: "What are we gaining? What are we getting from the irregularity that has characterized the school grounds within the last week, that will in any degree compensate for the amount of book study that we have lost?"

To my mind I do not believe that you have lost anything by the interruption. On the other hand, I am convinced that you have got the best kind of education. . . .

You have gained in this respect: in preparing for the reception and entertainment of the President of the United States and his Cabinet, and the distinguished persons who accompanied the party, you have had to do an amount of original thinking which you, perhaps, have never had to do before in your lives. You have been compelled to think; you have been compelled to put more than your bodily strength into what you have been doing. You could not have made the magnificent exhibition of our work which you have made if you had not been compelled to do original thinking and execution. Most of you never saw such an exhibition before; I never did. Those of you who had to construct floats that would illustrate our agriculture work and our mechanical and academic work, had to put a certain amount of original thought into the planning of these floats, in order to make them show the work to the best advantage; and two-thirds of you—yes, practically all of you—had never seen anything of the kind before. . . .

Education in the usual sense of the word is the mere committing to memory of something which has been known before us. Now during the last ten days we have had to solve problems of our own, not problems and puzzles that some one else originated for us. I do not believe that there is a person connected with the institution who is not stronger in mind, who is not more self-confident and self-reliant, so far as the qualities relate to what he is able to do with his mind or his hands, than he was ten or twelve days ago. There is the benefit that came to all of us. It put us to thinking and planning; it brought us in to contact with things that are out of the ordinary; and there is no education that surpasses this. I see more and more every year that the world is to be brought to the study of men and of things, rather than to the study of mere books. You will find more and more as the years go by, that people will gradually lay aside books, and study the nature of man in a way they have never done as yet. I tell you, then, that in this interruption of the regular school work you have not lost anything—you have gained; you have had your minds awakened, your faculties strengthened, and your hands guided. . . .

And so, as you go on, increasing your ability to do things of value, you will find that the problem which often now-a-days looks more and more difficult of solution will gradually become easier. . . . You will find it true, not only in this country but in other countries, that the demand will be more and more for people who can do something. Just in proportion as we can, as a race, get the reputation which I spoke to you about a few days ago, you will find there will be places for us. Regardless of colour or condition, the world is going to give the places of trust and remuneration to the men and women who can do a certain thing as well as anybody else or better. This is the whole problem. Shall we prepare ourselves to do something as well as anybody else or better? Just in proportion as we do this, you will find that nothing under the sun will keep us back.[4]

> **Washington pioneered the journey into the divide of racial boundaries established by man, not by God.**

This profound wisdom is such a powerful message for our educators and for parents as well. Washington encouraged his students to discover what was inside each one of them, what was in their heart, and to grow from potential to reality. His expectations were far above those of both his students and teachers because every day at Tuskegee was a step that had not been taken before. At Tuskegee, Dr. Washington pioneered the journey into the divide of racial boundaries that were established by man, not by God—all the while influencing those around him to do the same. To grow the heads, hands, and hearts of the students and their teachers, Washington established an environment of peace within the boundaries of Tuskegee Institute while what lurked on the outside was anything but peaceful.

In a separate message, Washington spoke these profound words about education and the experiment launched at Tuskegee.

> The value of the experiment made in Macon County is, in my opinion, less in the actual good that has been done to the twenty-six thousand people, white and black, who live there, than it is in the showing by actual experiment what a proper

system of Negro education can do in a country district toward solving the racial problem.

We have no race problem in Macon County; there is no friction between the races; agriculture is improving; the county is growing in wealth. In talking with the sheriff recently he told me that there is so little crime in this county that he scarcely finds enough to keep him busy. Furthermore, I think I am perfectly safe in saying that the white people in this county are convinced that Negro education pays.[5]

The advancement in overcoming the race problem at Tuskegee was the direct result of Booker T. Washington's design for education and growing in spirit by the grace of God. Through Dr. Washington, God provided a template revealing how to create a thriving environment within the boundaries of the institution. This template not only worked then; it can work again for an institution, church, school, as well as in the home. It is certainly a template we would do well to follow today. The environment inside the boundaries of Tuskegee was, by design, a place of freedom for the students, staff, and those who visited the campus. Tuskegee provided a place where those inside the boundaries were allowed to live and learn, protected from the ever-present dangers in rural Alabama.

Sadly, we failed to build on the wisdom and revelation of Washington's Tuskegee template. Those seeking to divide have had the upper hand over those whose desire is to unite. The success and grace of Dr. Washington has been buried in history, waiting for someone to replicate the Tuskegee template for education. We have a daunting task before us in terms of what America and her leaders will do with the growing number of immigrants crossing our borders in search of hope. Will they find hope here? Time will tell. Who knows, maybe someone will read this and rise up with a plan for the "proper system" as Washington described it. Is such an idea feasible and even possible? I believe it is, but there is something that will be required to execute such an idea. We must do it together. "Together," and only together—with all races working for a greater good—will it ever come to fruition. This would be the greatest example of racial harmony the world has ever seen. This is grace, and it is critical to peace on earth. The world is watching.

Education is the passport to the future,
for tomorrow belongs to those who prepare for it today.
—Malcolm X

Chapter Six

Character Grace

*Character-building is the Alpha and Omega
of all that Tuskegee stands for.*
—Emmett J. Scott, Washington's Executive Secretary

Booker T. Washington was more interested in the character of a man or woman than in the color of their skin. Every Sunday evening, Tuskegee students and faculty would gather for chapel service to hear Washington. He said this regarding these Sunday evening messages, "I have attempted from week to week to speak straight to the hearts of our students and teachers and visitors concerning the problems and questions that confront them in their daily life here in the South."[1] These messages were compiled in a book titled *Character Building*. As I read each one, I was amazed by what a great tool they are for parents to teach character. Building the character of our sons and daughters is essential to the process of becoming responsible as a man, husband, father, as a woman, wife, mother, as a good employee, employer, citizen, and neighbor. There is much to learn from these weekly messages, in both wisdom and attitude. These hidden treasures help us realize that the education of our sons and daughters is more than book knowledge. It is teaching them principles in preparation for life and the obstacles that lie ahead. Returning character building to our homes and the American classroom could be the beginning of restoring our identity as a civilized and educated people.

Dr. Washington's character and lessons in his Sunday evening messages were drawn largely from the Bible. He was committed to living and leading according to biblical principles. The following definition of biblical character is borrowed from Dr. Kathy Koch's book *Parent Differently: Raise Kids with Biblical Character That Changes Culture*:

> Biblical character is based on righteous qualities, virtuous standards, and irrefutable principles found in the Bible. . . . Biblical character marks us when we are humbly obedient to the Bible's Truth. . . . Biblical character is perfected as we develop a biblical worldview and our faith, love, wisdom, and obedience matures.[2]

One of the amazing messages Dr. Washington delivered to the students at Tuskegee made a distinct difference between the dark side and the bright side of life. The following words demonstrate his effectiveness as a communicator, his brilliance as a teacher, and his heart for the students and teachers he served.

Two Sides of Life

There are quite a number of divisions into which life can be divided, but for the purposes of this evening I am going to speak of two; the bright side of life and the dark side.

In thought, in talk, in action, I think you will find that you can separate life into these two divisions—the dark side and the bright side, the discouraging side and the encouraging side. You will find, too, that there are two classes of people, just as there are two divisions of the subject. There is one class that is schooling itself, and constantly training itself, to look upon the dark side of life; and there is another class, made up of people who are, consciously or unconsciously, constantly training themselves to look upon the bright side of life.

Now it is not wise to go too far in either direction. The person who schools himself to see the dark side of life is likely to make a mistake, and the person who schools himself to look only upon the bright side of life, forgetting all else, also is apt to make a mistake.

Notwithstanding this, l think l am right in saying that the persons who accomplish most in this world, those to whom on account of their helpfulness the world looks most for service—those who are most useful in every way—are those who are constantly seeing and appreciating the bright side as well as the dark side of life. . . .

l want you to go out from this institution so trained and so developed that you will be constantly looking for the bright, encouraging and beautiful things in life. It is the weak individual, as a rule, who is constantly calling attention to the other side—to the dark and discouraging things of life. When you go into your classrooms, l repeat, try to forget and overlook any weak points that you may think you see. Remember, and dwell upon, the consideration that has been given to the lesson, the faithfulness with which it was prepared, and the earnestness with which it is presented. Try to recall and to remember every good thing and every encouraging thing which has come under your observation, whether it has been in the classroom, or in the shop, or in the field. No matter where you are, seize hold on the encouraging things with which you come in contact. . . .

Try to get into a frame of mind where you will be constantly seeing and calling attention to the strong and beautiful things which you observe in the life and work of your teachers. Grow into the habit of talking about the bright side of life. . . . Just in proportion as you do this, you will find that you will not only influence yourself in the right direction, but that you will also influence others that way. . . .

It is often very easy to influence others in the wrong direction, and to grow into such a moody fault-finding disposition that one not only is miserable and unhappy himself, but makes every one with whom he comes in contact miserable and unhappy. The persons who live constantly in a fault-finding atmosphere, who see only the dark side of life, become negative characters. They are the people who never go forward. They never suggest a line of activity. They live simply on the negative side of life. Now, as students, you cannot afford to grow in that way. We want to send each one of you out from here, not as a negative force, but as a strong, positive, helpful force in the world. You will not accomplish the task which we expect of you if you go with a moody, discouraged, fault-finding disposition. To do the most that lies in you, you must go with a heart and head full of hope and faith in the world, believing that there is work for you to do, believing that you are the person to accomplish that work, and the one who is going to accomplish it.

In nine cases out of ten, the person who cultivates the habit of looking on the dark side of life is the little person, the miserable person, the one who is weak in mind, heart, and purpose. On the other hand, the person who cultivates the habit of looking on the bright side of life, and who calls attention to the beautiful and encouraging things in life is, in nine cases out of ten, the strong individual, the one to whom the world goes for intelligent advice and support. l am trying to get you to see, as students, the best things in life. Do not be satisfied with second-hand or third-hand things in life. Do not be satisfied until you have put yourselves into that atmosphere where you can seize and hold on to the very highest and most beautiful things that can be got out of life.[3]

Dr. Washington's legacy is more than history; it is a template that we should follow for personal development and collectively for simply getting along with each other. He was able to overcome inconceivable obstacles to influence and unite people in the community of Tuskegee, Macon County, and the state of Alabama. He possessed the same influence in the lofty corridors of American politics, in business, and in the hearts of all who called him friend. His humility was sincere and served to disarm some of his harshest detractors. One of his addresses beautifully illustrates his heart:

One of the highest ambitions of every man leaving Tuskegee Institute should be to help the people of his race find bottom—find bed rock—and then help them to stand upon that foundation. If we who are interested in the school can help you to do this, we shall count ourselves satisfied. And until the bed-rock of our life is found, and until we are planted thereon, all else is but plaster, but make-believe, but the paper on the walls of a house without framework. . . .

But to do this we must take advantage of the forces at hand. We must stand upon our own feet, and not upon a foundation supplied by another. We must begin our growth where our civilization finds us, and not try to begin on some other civilization.

If one race of people, or one individual, is simply to follow in the steps of another, no progress would ever be possible in the world. Let us remember that no other race of people ever had just such a problem to work out as we have. . . .

Show me the race that leads in work in wood and in metal, in the building of houses and factories, and in the constructing and operating of machinery, and I will show you the race that in the long run moulds public thought, that controls government, that leads in commerce, in the sciences, in the arts and in the professions.

What we should do in all our schools is to turn out fewer job-seekers and more job-makers. Any one can seek a job, but it requires a person of rare ability to create a job.

If it may seem to some of you that what I have been saying overlooks the development of the race in morals, ethics, religion and statesmanship, my answer would be this. You might as well argue that because a tree is planted deep down in Mother Earth, because it comes in contact with clay, and rock, and sand, and water, that through its graceful branches, its beautiful leaves and its fragrant blossoms it teaches no lesson of truth, beauty and divinity. You cannot plant a tree in air and have it live. Try it. No matter how much we may praise its proportions and enjoy its beauty, it dies unless its roots and fibres touch and have their foundation in

Mother Earth. What is true of the tree is true of a race.[4]

> *A people without the knowledge of their*
> *past history, origin, and culture*
> *is like a tree without roots.*
> —Marcus Garvey

Dr. Washington's commitment to truth and his methods at Tuskegee worked, and they can work today in our schools, our churches, and—where we need them most—our homes. His heart was genuine, his love real, and his grace was as powerful as it was humble. We are at a crossroads in American racial relations today. We can choose to emulate and elevate those who seek to divide us, or we can follow the lead of Booker T. Washington down a path of forgiveness, grace, and faith.

Simplicity

The simple truth is Dr. Washington was full of mercy and grace, and kept the main thing the main thing. Because he was secure in knowing his true identity, he would not let the realities of racial strife determine his future. He was, perhaps, the greatest leader of the Black community of his time, and of all times. But he was humble and embraced a can-do attitude that was steadfast and simple.

> When I speak of humbleness and simplicity, I do not mean that it is necessary for us to lose sight of what the world calls manhood and womanhood; that it is necessary to be cringing and unmanly; but you will find, in the long run, that the people who have the greatest influence in the world are the humble and simple ones. . . .

We want to be sure that in every industry, in every department of the institution, there is simplicity, humbleness, thoroughness. Whatever is entrusted to you to do in the industrial departments, in the class rooms, be sure that you put your whole heart into that thing. . . .

You want to be very sure, too, that as you go out into the world, you go out not ashamed to work; not ashamed to put in practice what you have learned here. As I come in contact with our graduates, I am very glad to be able to say that in almost no instance have I found a student who has been at Tuskegee long enough to learn the ways of the institution, or a graduate who has been ashamed to use his hands. Now that reputation we want to keep up. We want to be sure that such a reputation as this follows every student who goes out. . . .

There is great power in simplicity, simplicity of speech, simplicity of life in every form. The world has no patience with people who are superficial, who are trying to show off, who are trying to be what the world knows they are not. . . .

No one can in any way permanently hold back a race of people who are getting those elements of strength which the world recognizes, which the world has always recognized, and which it always will recognize, as indicating the highest type of manhood and womanhood. There is nothing, then, to be discouraged about. We are going forward, and we shall keep going forward if we do not let these difficulties which sometimes occur discourage us. You will find that every man and every woman who is worthy to be respected and praised and recognized will be respected and praised and recognized.[5]

Growth

Dr. Washington lived out his faith. He lived out his commitment to unity. He relentlessly pursued a dream where all races lived in harmony. He was always growing. In his words:

> I want to impress upon you this evening the importance of continued growth. I very much wish that each one of you might imagine, this evening, your father and your mother to be looking at you and examining into every act of your life while here. I wish that you might feel, as it were, their very heart throbs. I wish that you might realize, perhaps as you have never realized before, how anxious they are that you should succeed here. I wish that you could know how many prayers they send up, day after day, that your school life may be more and more successful as one day succeeds another, that you may grow to be successful, studious, strong men and women, who will reflect credit upon yourselves and honour upon your families. . . .
>
> I want you to resolve that you are going to put into this year the hardest and the most earnest work that you have ever done in your life, to resolve that this is going to be the greatest, the most courageous and the most sinless year of life that you have ever lived; I want you to make up your minds to do this; to decide that you are going to continually grow— and grow more tomorrow than today. There are but two directions in this life in which you can grow; backward or forward. You can grow stronger, or you can grow weaker; you can grow greater, or smaller; but it will be impossible for you to stand still. . . .
>
> I hope you are learning that labour with the

hand, in any form whatever, is not disgraceful. I hope that you are learning, day by day, that all kinds of labour whether—whether with the mind or with the hand—are honourable, and that people only disgrace themselves by being and keeping in idleness. . . .

I want to emphasize the fact that we want you to grow in the direction of character—to grow stronger each day in the matter of character. When I say character, here, I mean to use the word in its broadest sense. The institution wants to find you growing more polite to your fellows every day, as you come in contact with them, whether it be in the classroom, in the shop, in the field, in the dining room, or in your bedroom. No matter where you are, I want you to find yourselves growing more polite and gentlemanly. Notice I do not say merely that I want your teachers—those who are over you—to find you growing more polite; I want you to find yourselves so. If you are not doing this, you are going backward, you are going in the wrong direction.

I want to find you each day more thoughtful of others, and less selfish. I want you to be more conscientious in your thoughts and in your work, and with regard to your duty toward others. This is growing in the right direction; not doing this is growing in the wrong direction. Nor do I want you to feel that you are to strive for this spirit of growth for this one year alone, or for the time that you are here. I hope that you will continue to grow in the forward direction. . . .

We want Tuskegee students to go out from here and establish homes that will be models in every respect for those about them—homes that will show that the lives of the persons who have established them are models for the lives of those who live about them. If you do this, your lives are going to be a constant going forward; for, I repeat, your lives are going to be one thing or the other, continually going backward or continually going forward.[6]

Finally, as we follow the legacy of Dr. Washington and pursue a path to racial harmony, we once again can learn from the call to be more childlike. Washington used to address his students midyear with words to exhort and encourage them. Life was not easy for students at Tuskegee due to strict academic standards and the realities of racial strife in the latter years of the nineteenth century and the early twentieth century in the deep South. One semester, he shared these heartfelt words of love and grace:

If you have not already done so—and I hope you have—I think that you will find this a convenient season for each one of you to stop and to consider your school year very carefully; to consider your life in school from every point of view; to place yourselves, as it were, in the presence of your parents, or your friends at home; to place yourselves in the presence of those who stand by and support this institution; to place yourselves in the presence of your teachers and of all who are in any way interested in you.

Now, suppose you were tonight sitting down by your parents' side, by their fireside, looking them in the face, or by the side of your nearest and dearest friends, those who have done the most for you, those who have stood by you most closely. Suppose you were in that position. I want to ask you to answer this question, In considering your school life—in your studies, for example—during the year, thus far, have you done your best?[7]

Individual Responsibility

Booker believed that a person was solely responsible for himself, whether providing a service for others or providing for the needs of himself and those who depended on him.

> I have referred in a general way, before this, when I have been speaking to you, to the fact that each one of you ought to feel an interest in whatever task is set you to do here over and above the mere bearing which that task has on your own life. I wish to speak more specifically tonight on this subject—on what I may term the importance of your feeling a sense of personal responsibility not only for the successful performance of every task set you, but for the successful outcome of every worthy undertaking with which you come in contact.
>
> You ought to realize that your actions will not affect yourselves alone. In this age it is almost impossible for a man to live for himself alone. On every side our lives touch those of others; their lives touch ours. Even if it were possible to live otherwise, few would wish to. A narrow life, a selfish life, is almost sure to be not only unprofitable but unhappy. The happy people and the successful people are those who go out of their way to reach and influence for good as many persons as they can. In order to do this, though, in order best to fit one's self to live this kind of life, it is important that

certain habits be acquired; and an essential one of these is the habit of realizing one's responsibility to others.

Your actions will affect other people in one way or another, and you will be responsible for the result. You ought always to remember this, and govern yourselves accordingly. . . .

The world is looking for men and women who can tell one why they can do this thing or that thing, how a certain difficulty was surmounted or a certain obstacle removed. But the world has little patience with the man or woman who takes no real interest in the performance of a duty, or who runs against a snag and gets discouraged, and then simply tells why he did not do a thing, and gives excuses instead of results. Opportunities never come a second time, nor do they wait for our leisure. The years come to us but once, and they come then only to pass swiftly on, bearing the ineffaceable record we have put upon them. If we wish to make them beautiful years or profitable years, we must do it moment by moment as they glide before us.[8]

Helping Others

Booker T. Washington lived daily to serve in one way or another. He always emphasized the value of helping others as being representative of the "Tuskegee spirit."

This institution does not exist for your education alone; it does not exist for your comfort and happiness altogether, although those things are important, and we keep them in mind; it exists that we may give you intelligence, skill of hand, and strength of mind and heart; and we help you in these ways that you, in turn, may help others. We help you that you may help somebody else, and if you do not do this, when you go out from here, then our work here has been in vain. . . .

There are people in the world who never think, who never map out anything for themselves, who have to wait to be told what to do. People of that kind are not worth anything. They really ought to pay rent for the air they breath[e], for they only vitiate it. Now we do not want such people as those here. We want people who are going to think, people who are going to prepare themselves. . . .

The most interesting thing connected with this institution is the magnificent record that our graduates are making. As the institution grows larger, we do not want to lose the spirit of self-sacrifice, the spirit of usefulness which the graduates and the students who have gone out from here have shown. We want you to help somebody else. We want you not to think of yourselves alone. The more you do to make somebody else happy, the more happiness will you receive in turn. If you want to be happy, if you want to live a contented life, if you want to live a life of genuine pleasure, do something for somebody else. When you feel unhappy, disagreeable and miserable, go to some one else who is miserable and do that person an act of kindness, and you will find that you will be made happy. The miserable persons in this world are the ones whose hearts are narrow and hard; the happy ones are those who have great big hearts. Such persons are always happy.[9]

I want you to go out into the world, not to have an easy time,
but to make sacrifices, and to help somebody else.

The Gospel of Service

Booker believed that God designs each race to excel in different
ways. He believed his people were gifted in a broad variety of
categories, setting no limits on what they could accomplish, given
the opportunity. The category of service is one in which he believed
his people excelled.

> The subject on which I am going to speak to you for
> a few minutes tonight, "The Gospel of Service," may
> not, when you first hear it, strike a very responsive
> chord in your hearts and minds, but I assure you I
> have nothing but the very highest and best interest
> of the race at heart when I select this subject to talk
> about.
>
> The word "service" has too often been
> misunderstood, and on this account it has in too
> many cases carried with it a meaning which indicates
> degradation. Every individual serves another in
> some capacity, or should do so. Christ said that
> he who would become the greatest of all must
> become the servant of all; that is, He meant that in
> proportion as one renders service he becomes great.
> The President of the United States is a servant of
> the people, because he serves them; the Governor
> of Alabama is a servant, because he renders service
> to the people of the State; the greatest merchant
> in Montgomery is a servant, because he renders
> service to his customers; the school teacher is a
> servant, because it is his duty to serve the best
> interests of his pupils; the cook is a servant, because

it is her duty to serve those for whom she works; the housemaid is a servant, because it is her duty to care for the property intrusted to her in the best manner in which she is able.

In one way or another, every individual who amounts to anything is a servant. The man or the woman who is not a servant is one who accomplishes nothing. It is very often true that a race, like an individual, does not appreciate the opportunities that are spread out before it until those opportunities have disappeared. Before us, as a race in the South today, there is a vast field for service and usefulness which is still in our hands, but which I fear will not be ours to the same extent very much longer unless we change our ideas of service, and put new life, put new dignity and intelligence into it. . . .

In too many cases, I fear, we use these occupations merely as stepping stones, holding on to them until we can find something else to do, in a careless and slipshod manner. We want to change all this, and put our whole souls into these occupations, and in a large degree make them our lifework. In proportion as we do this, we shall lay a foundation upon which our children and grandchildren are to rise to higher things. The foundation of every race must be laid in the common everyday occupations that are right about our doors. It should not be our thought to see how little we can put into our work, but how much; not how quickly we can get rid of our tasks, but how well we can do them.

I often wish that I had the means to put into every city a large training-school for giving instruction in all lines of domestic service. Few things would add more to the fundamental usefulness of the race than such a school. Perhaps it may be suggested that my argument has reference only to our serving white people. It has reference to doing whatever we do in the best manner, no matter whom we serve. The individual who serves a black man poorly will serve a white man poorly. . . .

Many white people seldom come in contact with the Negro in any other capacity than that of domestic service. If they get a poor idea of our character and service in that respect, they will infer that the entire life of the Negro is unsatisfactory from every point of view. We want to be sure that wherever our life touches that of the white man, we conduct ourselves so that he will get the best impression possible of us.

In spite of all the fault I have found, I would say this before I stop. I recognize that the people of no race, under similar circumstances, have made greater progress in thirty-five years than is true of the people of the Negro race. If I have spoken to you thus plainly and frankly, it is that our progress in the future may be still greater than it has been in the past.[10]

Serving one another in truth and spirit was bedrock in Dr. Washington's interpretation of himself and his race. Until we agree to serve as he did, always keeping our eye on the main thing, we will fall short of the spirit he described as the "Tuskegee spirit." I close this chapter with words borrowed from the book *Tuskegee and Its People: Their Ideals and Achievements*, by Booker T. Washington.

The school has sought from the very beginning to make itself of practical value to the Negro people and to the South as well. . . . It has sought to influence its young men and women to live unselfish, sacrificing lives; to put into practice the lessons taught on every side that make for practical, helpful every-day living. . . .

The object of the school is to train men and women who will go out and repeat the work done here, to teach what they have learned to others, and to leaven the whole mass of the Negro.[11]

Dr. Washington said the following in regard to the students who had graduated and moved on from Tuskegee:

I can not find a dozen former students in idleness. They are in shop, field, schoolroom, home, or the church. They are busy because they have placed themselves in demand by learning to do that which the world wants done, and because they have learned the disgrace of idleness and the sweetness of labor.[12]

The world will little note, nor long remember what we say here,
but it can never forget what they did here.
—Abraham Lincoln

PART III

Interpretation Grace

*Because of Dr. Washington's absolute faith in the possibilities of his
own race, because of his pride in his race, because he loved his race,
he analyzed and frankly interpreted the Negro to himself, telling him
his shortcomings and failings in unvarnished fashion, teaching him
what right education means and what it should do for the individual
and the race, working out in concrete form in Tuskegee Institute, as
well as outside of the institution, his ideas of education.*
—Robert Russa Moton

CHAPTER SEVEN

Kindred Hearts

*Friendship is not something you learn in schools. But if
you haven't learned the meaning of friendship,
you haven't really learned anything.*
—Muhammad Ali

Outside of his family, Robert Russa Moton knew Booker T. Washington, perhaps, better than anyone other than George Washington Carver. In addition to succeeding Washington as Principal of Tuskegee Institute, Moton followed a similar path through Hampton Institute. He also joined Washington on many trips throughout the South, where he spoke on behalf of the Black race and on the importance of education. They were friends and brothers in the great cause of interpreting their race to the world and navigating opportunities, though limited, that were to come with emancipation. Moton's words were profound in that Washington not only interpreted the Negro to himself, but he also interpreted the White race to his people—the good as well as the bad.

Perhaps the greatest outcome from my time in the classroom under the tutelage of Dr. Washington is how he helped me interpret myself, my shortcomings, and my prejudices through the filter of grace. He interpreted the White race to me, our shortcomings, weaknesses, and responsibility to be forthright in all matters, especially concerning what divides us. He challenged me to live and treat people like I believe that God is who He says He is and that Christ lives in me; anything that falls short of that is simply hypocrisy. This was a huge revelation for me and transformed my heart. Booker helped me see how we are all interconnected by the grace of God. We are one Blood among many nations. He made it clear that it is okay to be critical of ourselves and of our race, as long as those criticisms are purposed with changes that grow us toward, and not away from, God and each other.

As I look in the rearview mirror at where and how my Tuskegee journey began, I have to ask myself some questions: What now? What am I going to do with what I know regarding how our journey as a nation could have been different had we followed the path blazed by Booker T. Washington and his cohorts? What will you do now that you know the truth?

Every race is uniquely different, even more so than the colors of our skin. It is especially critical that in our differences we get serious about grace. The truth is, none of us has anything that makes us better than the next person. Sin separates us in countless ways, and the color of our skin is just one of those. It is, however, our first impression of each other, unless we make it not so. Truth is, it is time for us to get over ourselves and replace race with grace. It is time for us all, together, to forgive, have mercy, and see beyond the appearance of each other to the invisible qualities in the heart.

I learned so much from Booker T. Washington's immutable life lessons, but to a greater degree from his deep well of wisdom and knowledge regarding the human condition. Washington helped me learn to see people beyond their appearance, beyond first impressions, to what lies underneath the skin God gave them. You rarely hear the word *discernment* in our world today, perhaps because there's just not a lot of it going on. Discernment is recognizing truth when you see it, and equally as important is to recognize the distortion of truth, which pervades our world. That is what I hope you take away from *Critical Grace*.

Throughout my Tuskegee journey there have been an untold number of revelations down to bedrock, but when I reread the words, "He analyzed and frankly interpreted the Negro to himself, telling him his shortcomings and failures in unvarnished fashion,"[1] the light of bedrock truth came on so brightly, it about blinded me. What I realized is that Booker gave us the answer to our race problem. He not only interpreted himself and his race, but he interpreted the White race. He knew the White race better than White people.

I now know why I have friends of color—not because my little circle of friends passes DEI requirements, but so they can help me interpret myself, as a man of the White race. They help me see my shortcomings and lack of understanding, not only of myself but of other races. This revelation may not move the needle of racial harmony for you one iota, but for me, it is life-changing.

Critical grace is applying the wisdom of God to see beyond the color of one's skin and discerning what is real in a world that calls good things bad and bad things good. We must be critical of ourselves and how we relate to others if we are serious about living life on the bright side and standing against evil. The prophet Isaiah spoke to this when he wrote, "Woe to those who call evil good, and good evil; who put darkness for light, and light for darkness; who put bitter for sweet, and sweet for bitter! Woe to those who are wise in their own eyes, and prudent in their own sight!" (Isaiah 5:20-21).

This part consists of thoughts that turned into sentences, sentences into paragraphs, paragraphs into articles, and articles into chapters. My request is that you try not to follow a determined narrative through this part but allow each piece to stand alone while pointing to one thing: truth according to Gospel of Jesus Christ. If my words speak to some corner of your spirit, simply smile and praise the One who made you.

CHAPTER EIGHT

Truth Is Grace

*We work the truth into our lives and bodies to replace the assumptions
and practices that we have acquired through years of malformation.*
—David Takle

This third part is a collection of the realities that resulted from
my reading Booker T. Washington. I learned so much about
discerning truth from his immutable life lessons, but to a greater
degree, Washington helped me see beyond the obvious, down
to bedrock, which is essential in seeing others as God sees them.
Equally as important is learning to discern when truth is being
distorted or spun. That is what I hope you take away from this part
of *Critical Grace*.

The following quote by Dr. Carol Swain speaks to the open
dialogue we need for the greatest outcome of closing the gap that
divides us.

> One of the most urgent things we need to do is
> create situations where honest dialogue can take
> place among people who ordinarily avoid one
> another. The most critical problems impacting our
> nation and African Americans in particular will not
> be solved by like-minded people conversing with
> one another.[1]

Dr. Swain is spot-on in describing how we accomplish nothing when we fail to include those who have a difference of opinion. Dr. Swain knows from experience, and she is an honest woman who speaks truth, even when it is painful. Refusing to be a victim, she has experienced a life ascent from the bottom to a place of prominence and success. She started life in poverty, dropped out of middle school, married at age sixteen, and had three children before she turned twenty-one. Because she had a can-do attitude and a winsome spirit, she flourished, not allowing her circumstances in life to determine the outcome. Dr. Swain is a grace-filled woman and speaks of how essential attitude is to success in life. Her faith is grounded in biblical truth. Her statement is true and calls us to a place of humble resolve to be gracious yet critical, and she is absolutely correct when she says our problems will not be solved by people who agree with each other. We need each other, and our differences, for the debate that leads to the truth that will set us free. For someone to disagree is actually a blessing because we all need others to help us evaluate how we are answering the tough questions in life. We are better together, even in our differences.

We Press On

The following writings are outcomes of my Tuskegee journey. They were not on my list of topics to write about but were revealed along the way. As I studied Booker T. Washington, I also read books by men and women smarter than me, like Carol Swain and Shelby Steele. Grace is critical to every nook and cranny of our mind because grace is the manifest presence of God. Grace is critical to hearing from the One who made us, and then interpreting what we hear about ourselves and the world around us, even in our brokenness. Critical grace helps us interpret what is true and what isn't from the voices we hear, and that includes our own.

A lie doesn't become truth, wrong doesn't become right,
and evil doesn't become good, just because it's accepted by a majority.
—Booker T. Washington

Critical Grace Is No Theory

Critical grace is the ability to interpret accurately what is good when the world is calling it bad, and bad when the world calls it good. We must be critical thinkers if we are serious about living life on the bright side and standing guard against evil's assault.

The brilliance and wisdom of Booker T. Washington may be more relevant today than at any other time in history. We have digressed in so many ways, but above all in common sense and rational thought. To be called a racist in today's culture is almost a compliment, because for the most part the racist label is being used against the moral authority of God. Cancel culture and woke ideology can be included in the intentional pursuit of destroying men and women of high moral character simply because their ideology leans more into God than the world. If Booker T. Washington were alive today, he would be called Uncle Tom or the Black face of White supremacy. We have flipped the script from being led by wise and stable-minded men and women to being led by unstable and confused adolescents in the bodies of adults. Imperial facts mean nothing, nor does learning from history in an economy opposed to God.

Facts are stubborn things; and whatever may be our wishes,
our inclinations, or the dictates of our passions,
they cannot alter the state of facts and evidence.
—John Adams

Cancel culture is the elevation of ignorance over knowledge and has become the irrational way for immature and weak-minded people to manipulate their beliefs so the masses are ignorant of moral truth. They proclaim their way as right and control the false narrative of a self-proclaimed righteousness. Immature adults who believe they have cornered the market on all things appropriate—canceling freedom of speech and freedom of choice—are a cancer to a culture that is already confused. It is a "because I said so" mentality driven by a godless worldview. Through mainstream media we are being led to believe things that are simply not true, and to believe anything else is an abomination to the elite power hustlers and race-baiters. The sad thing is, most Americans have little or no information to push back against these lies, so they go along believing nonsense from the "intellectuals" who have no idea what it means to think critically and independently.

Another new word has been introduced by a confused culture that has an agenda to ensure that victimhood remains active in every aspect of our culture. "Wokeness" has become the rallying cry of the victim and is the antithesis of truth, maturity, and wisdom according to God. Born out of political correctness, the whole "woke" ideology is an attempt to compensate for the void in the minds of the clueless. These irrational individuals who can only make it in life by making themselves victims of someone or something have no intention of living with a work ethic as responsible citizens, serving a greater good of any kind.

Wokeness opposes facts, function, and basic common sense. For example, in a course on racism from our church, the facilitator made the statement that if you are White and you do not have a Black doctor, you should have one. I would never be opposed to having a Black doctor, but to select a doctor simply because he is Black is absurd. As a matter of fact, my retina specialist is Black, but he is not my doctor because he is Black. He is my doctor because he is the best retina specialist in the city. He just happens to be Black. The whole idea of placing someone in a position simply because of the color of their skin or their gender identity and not because they are the best qualified person for the job is insane and describes the insanity of the woke narrative.

The latest and perhaps the most destructive initiative is DEI. Diversity-Equity-Inclusion is another affirmative action that is designed for optics only. DEI does nothing to provide opportunities for a fair and balanced learning or work environment. What it does is open the door for hiring individuals based on identity and not merit. Grace is critical in seeing through to the true purpose of such initiatives, which drive an agenda to manipulate power.

> *If the map doesn't agree with*
> *the ground, the map is wrong.*
> —Gordon Livingston

This should not surprise us. When our schools become institutions of indoctrination, we should expect distortions of truth regarding what is good for the education and training of our children and what is not. Wokeness is nothing more than the methods being used to silence the voices of the people who have authority in the lives of kids, the parents. It's the narrative of depraved minds that thrive on the idea of creating a generation of sexually confused young adults. It is what people do when the authority under which they live is evil. Instead of allowing different opinions in a civilized debate, they simply cancel you because their argument is baseless and makes no sense. Common sense is uncommon to these people, so they find a way to put a label on you. You're a racist, a homophobe, or some other nonsensical label. Words like *character*, *courage*, *integrity*, and *joy* are offensive to these cotton-headed ninny muggins who live in denial that God even exists.

Booker T. Washington was prophetic when he spoke the following words:

> There is another class of coloured people who make
> a business of keeping the troubles, the wrongs, and
> the hardships of the Negro race before the public.

Having learned that they are able to make a living out of their troubles, they have grown into the settled habit of advertising their wrongs—partly because they want sympathy and partly because it pays. Some of these people do not want the Negro to lose his grievances, because they [do] not want to lose their jobs.[2]

Booker's words are spot-on in describing the rallying cry of the woke mob. Making themselves the victims of those who live victoriously is a way of life and a means of making a living. These people are not ignorant; they are simply misled and have no clue how to think critically with grace. However, be encouraged that when the light comes on for one of these idiots, he is hooked for life by the light.

> *Egotism is the anesthetic that dulls*
> *the pain of stupidity.*
> —Booker T. Washington

God made each one of us in His image but uniquely different. He also provides the grace to live in community with those differences. Remember, God is love, and love abounds in His grace according to the Gospel. God created us with different colors of skin so that by grace He can magnify Himself when we come together in spite of the divide. Our likeness is in Him. It is in our differences, talents, skills, opportunities, and heritage (which includes the color of our skin) that God reveals His grace in racial harmony. He purposed each of us to serve Him first, and then serve those in the world around us. Racial harmony is an inside job.

In order to experience unity in our country, it is critical to receive the grace of God for the sins of our past and to forgive each other. Grace is critical to how we engage with each other, regardless of the color of our skin. Remember the song we sang growing up? "Jesus loves the little children, all the children of the world. Red and yellow, black and white, they are precious in His sight. Jesus loves the little children of the world."[3] This simple little song carries the narrative to love everyone like Jesus, because we are all siblings in the family of God. Every single one of us is challenged when it comes to grace. Our behavior toward one another is an outpouring of what is in our hearts and what we believe. It is all grace because it is all God, whether we choose to believe it or not. The time for grace is now, and it is critical. The following words spoken by Voddie Baucham put in perspective the idolatry of skinfullness.

> As a believer, I came to a crossroad, and I recognized that, for the most part, I identified a lot more with my blackness than I did with my Christianity. For the most part, it was much more important to me that I was black than it was that I was a Christian. Over time, I had to come to grips with the fact that in Christ, at the foot of the Cross, there is no male or female, there is no Jew or Greek, slave or free. Over time, I had to come to grips with the fact that Christ died, not only to reconcile us vertically to the Father, but to reconcile us horizontally with one another. I am a member of the body of Christ, and nothing supersedes that. Nothing is more important than that.[4]

Your ways and your doings have procured these things for you. This is your wickedness, because it is bitter, because it reaches to your heart.
—Jeremiah 4:18

Lighten Up

While this Voddie Baucham quote is fresh in our minds, I thought it might be fun to do a little word swapping to move us closer to who we truly are. Pastor Baucham's quote is a good template for each one of us in determining the reality of who we are and who we are becoming. We are either Black or Christian, White or Christian, Hispanic or Christian, Asian or Christian, all other ethnicities or Christian, churchgoer or Christian, agnostic or believer, in bondage or emancipated. Like Pastor Baucham, we must all come to grips with who we are—by God's definition and not our own. Either we are true to our identity in Christ or we are not. Either we will say nothing supersedes that or we will not. To get down to the bedrock of who we really are, let's do some self-evaluating and fill in some rather self-exposing blanks. Be as honest as you can when filling in the blanks with whatever is at the top of who you are. Our purpose in this exercise is to identify your greatest passions and to make you aware of who you are and who you are becoming.

> As a believer, I came to a crossroad, and I recognized that, for the most part, I identified a lot more with my_____ than I did with my Christianity. For the most part, it was much more important to me that I was _____than it was that I was a Christian. Over time, I had to come to grips with the fact that in Christ, at the foot of the Cross, there is no male or female, there is no Jew or Greek, slave or free. Over time, I had to come to grips with the fact that Christ died, not only to reconcile us vertically to the Father, but to reconcile us horizontally with one another. I am a member of the body of Christ, and nothing supersedes that. Nothing is more important than that.

Baucham's statement hits closer to home than most of us want to admit. When we are honest and fill in the blanks with our own idols, it is uncomfortable but can be liberating if we allow the unconditional love of God to draw us in. I have read this quote to many people, and without exception, they agree that we all—not just Blacks—must to come to grips with what we truly idolize. Whether it is racial prejudice, lust, sexual perversion, greed, or self-righteousness, we either come clean and fill in the blanks accordingly or hide behind a fig leaf like Adam and Eve when their sin was exposed in the garden.

In Matthew 11:30, Jesus said, "For My yoke is easy and My burden is light." The question is, do we truly believe it? Do we really believe that the brokenness, the suffering, and the way we treat each other can actually be made easier? Absolutely it can, because of what Jesus did on the cross and because we have a choice in the matter. It all depends on how we choose to release our grip on the stronghold of entitlement. It is in our nature to believe this way, and it is in the nature of God to lighten that burden through the finished work of Jesus Christ. He paid the debt for all sin, so you and I can forgive each others past, present, and future.

It's a choice we make every day in one way or another. Either you face the day, never giving thought to lightening up on the people around you, especially your offenders, or you choose to navigate the day with a forgiving spirit, living the words of Jesus, allowing Him to make your yoke easy and your burdens light. We can choose to hold on tight like it's the last piece of chicken at Babe's, or we can lighten up and share the goodness around the table of life.

How strong is a faith that can't stand up to a few honest questions?
—Kenneth C. Davis

Case in Point

Michigan was gearing up to face Alabama in the Rose Bowl on New Year's Day 2024. Michigan offensive coordinator Sherrone Moore was criticized for how he answered a rather stupid question from a reporter regarding the viability of Alabama quarterback Jalen Milroe. The question was rooted in race, and Sherrone's answer was rooted in grace. He said, "Really, I don't see color. My wife is Caucasian. My kids are mixed. I deal with black, white. I've lived in Kansas where you can be in the house with the door open at 12, and in New Jersey where you have to be in the house by 6 o'clock. I've seen all cards of the spectrum."[5] Sherrone's response drove people crazy and lit up social media with some of the most idiotic responses. It is amazing that people who love and revere MLK forget his dream and live their lives embittered by his ideology of character over skin. This is just another attempt from the media to keep the fire of racial bitterness burning in the hearts of Americans.

The question Sherrone Moore was asked is typical of someone who is either ignorant or simply enjoys the power they wield in the distortion of how far America has come. These types are divisive to the core and must be called out. Sherrone's answer was seasoned with grace. Sherrone has a resemblance to Booker T. Washington that is more than skin deep. Sherrone is an influencer and an emancipated man who sees as God sees.

Moral Authority

Booker T. Washington was a visionary. He could foresee the potential for his race because of the opportunities resulting from emancipation. Though these opportunities would be limited, to a large degree, because White supremacy was the order of the day, they were nonetheless real. Although he was an influential leader of the Black race, he had limited moral authority outside the boundaries of Tuskegee. He was adept at identifying any and every opportunity to service and better himself and became an exceptional fundraiser for Tuskegee. He cultivated relationships with philanthropic Whites who supported his efforts at Tuskegee, men like Andrew Carnegie and Julius Rosenwald, not to mention Presidents Woodrow Wilson, Grover Cleveland, William H. Taft, and Teddy Roosevelt.

Dr. Washington never believed that he was a victim or that fate had been sealed for him, or his race, simply because they had been born Black. Had he possessed the moral authority that Blacks have today, his influence would have been vilified because his ideology was grounded in the biblical truth. Because Booker was Black, he was not taken seriously among many Whites. At the same time, many of his own race chose to disregard him because he was a man who believed in cooperating with Whites in hard work and equality of opportunities, not equality of outcomes. These virtues of Booker T. Washington reminded his people too much of the White man, so they opposed him and his ideology of self-reliance.

America lost an opportunity to blaze a path of racial harmony through the legacy of Dr. Washington and lead her citizens forward to peace among her mosaic of nations. Government has a tendency to lead us away from principles that unite and instead follow those that keep us divided. It is in our nature to turn a deaf ear to authority that is grounded in the moral authority of God. We like to follow our own bents, and with a mainstream media that pulls us away from God's order of morality, distortion of truth is the native language. It seems division is more newsworthy in their eyes than to simply report the news. Not to get too political, but the party of slavery, the Democrat party, has perfected this technique of promising and never delivering. Rhetoric without remedies is the strategy of those who want to lead us away from real solutions for our people and what divides us. Those with real solutions are often silenced.

> **Mr. Moynihan's report was swept under the rug.**

The Democrat Party did this to one of their own, Daniel Patrick Moynihan, just one year after President Lyndon B. Johnson signed into law the Civil Rights Act of 1964. Mr. Moynihan wrote a report on poverty in America, known as the Moynihan Report. Because it didn't fit the victimhood narrative of the Democrats, Mr. Moynihan's report was swept under the rug. At the time Moynihan was Assistant Secretary of Labor under President Johnson. Following are a few paragraphs taken from "The Negro Family: The Case for National Action":

> At the heart of the deterioration of the fabric of Negro society is the deterioration of the Negro family.
>
> It is the fundamental source of the weakness of the Negro community at the present time. . . .
>
> The role of the family in shaping character and ability is so pervasive as to be easily overlooked. The family is the basic social unit of American life; it is the basic socializing unit. By and large, adult conduct in society is learned as a child. . . .
>
> But there is one truly great discontinuity in family structure in the United States at the present time: that between the white world in general and that of the Negro American.[6]

Moynihan, whom later became a senator, was prophetic in terms of the breakdown of the family and the future of Blacks in America. Had the government chosen to support the findings of the report, they would have led the way in helping educate and train men and women of the Black race industrially and academically to learn how to be independent and reliable citizens. But because the report argued that the single-parent Black family was becoming more common, and that these mom-led families were not the product of unemployment but because the party of slavery wanted to keep Blacks enslaved to government dependence, this truth in Moynihan's report went nowhere.

> **By and large, adult conduct in society is learned as a child.**

How often do we hear the reason so many young Black men are either in prison or end up dead is a result of Black-on-Black crime? It is the same reason Daniel Patrick Moynihan pointed out in his report to the government in 1965. The family unit was being destroyed, and they were growing up without a father in the home. Sadly, nothing has changed, and this remains true today for both Backs and Whites just as it was in 1965. The bold headings below are from the Moynihan Report, which further point out the dilemma Blacks were facing and continue to face today. Under each of the headings there is more text that you can read online.

By contrast, the family structure of lower-class Negroes is highly unstable, and in many urban centers is approaching complete breakdown.

Nearly a Quarter of Urban Negro Marriages are Dissolved.

Almost One-Fourth of Negro Families are Headed by Females.

The Breakdown of the Negro Family Has Led to a Startling Increase in Welfare Dependency.[7]

There was one problem with this timely and accurate report written by Daniel Patrick Moynihan. He was White, and because America was being transformed from White supremacy to White guilt, Whites no longer possessed the moral authority they controlled under the tyranny of White supremacy. Anything a White man or woman said was not to be trusted and considered racist. Moynihan genuinely cared for what was happening to Black families but had little to no support from Whites in general, especially from his party.

So here we are. We missed the visionary wisdom of Booker T. Washington, who was not only a brilliant leader but possibly the greatest ever trophy of the Constitution. He gave us Tuskegee Institute, perhaps the greatest expression of the grace of God on American soil, not to mention a proven template for how school, home, and even a country should be stewarded. He cared deeply for his race but also for Whites and Native Americans as well. But Booker T. Washington had one problem: he was Black.

> He cared deeply for his race but also for Whites as well.

Then, our mindless leaders pooh-poohed on Daniel Patrick Moynihan's report that may have saved Black and poor families in general from being destroyed, encouraging more fathers to remain in the home, but Moynihan was White. Two men—one Black and one White—both denied, yet both would have had greater influence had they lived in the other one's era. Could they have swapped places in time, Washington would have moral authority today and would not be as opposed because he is Black. Booker would be called "Uncle Tom" today because his methods call for self-reliance and hard work versus dependence on government. Both men most certainly would have been opposed by the party known for rhetoric that tickles the ears but does little to lift up the man farthest down.

CHAPTER NINE

Common Grace

Grace is for life, not just for forgiveness.
—Jim Wilder, *Renovated*

Uncommon Common Ground

If you happen to be Catholic, an extra measure of grace for the writer is required as you read on. In my first book, *Narrowtive*, I wrote a little story titled "Baptist Catholics." That label was bestowed upon a Catholic friend by another friend who is evangelical. Their offices are close to each other, and the Catholic attends and sometimes leads a weekly Bible study at the office of the evangelical. When we gather as children of God, we are on common ground.

> *Pray that we will keep the common ground.*
> *Won't you pray for me, and I'll pray for you.*
> —Michael W. Smith, "Pray for Me"

I have quite a few Catholic friends. Over the past several years, I have had the privilege of attending some Catholic men's events. The messages taught and the themes of these gatherings are, in large part, no different from the gatherings of evangelicals, other than Mass and the recitations. The bottom line is, when we come together as sons of the living God, we are united in heart and of one

Spirit. When people ask me how I came to have so many Catholic friends, my simple answer is "grace." God has graced me with rich friendships that vary in how each one interprets Scripture, yet we are the same under God. We agree on the main things and have grace for each other in areas where we may not agree. We are the same in the eyes of God, and the Scripture that helps me keep the main thing the main thing is in the last book of the Old Testament. It reads as follows: "Do we not all have one Father? Did not one God create us? Why do we profane the covenant of our ancestors by being unfaithful to one another?" (Malachi 2:10, NIV).

In context, Malachi was speaking to the entirety—all tribes, all factions—of the children of Israel. While they were all recipients of the covenant God made with Moses under the old law, they were human and had differences in how they interpreted God's Word. I am taking some liberty here to use this place in time and the clarity with which Malachi spoke to make a point. The message is specific to the children of Israel under the old covenant, but it certainly applies to us today in the context of racial harmony. While we have major differences, both individually and collectively, we are all created in the image of God, and we now live under the new covenant that Jesus established on the cross. His grace is the solution to moving forward together, keeping the main thing the main thing. It is only at the foot of the cross that we will find common ground—and that is in the resurrected Jesus. It is critical that we surrender our racial strongholds for grace.

> Seeing those around us as God sees them is essential to peace on earth.

Our problem is that we forget what is most important. We get drawn into conversations that require taking sides in matters that are not essential to the most important thing we have in common—God. If you will do this one thing, you will be amazed at how much better you get along with people. You will also see more clearly how Jesus sees people. Seeing those around us as He sees them is essential to peace on earth. As you grow in your comprehension of grace, you will be more at peace. My friend David Holland offers a "cast down your bucket where you are" phrase that sounds like something Booker would say: "Humility and a heart of gratitude are key to a lifestyle of power-filled rest."[1]

I tend to believe that Booker was familiar with Malachi 2:10. He certainly lived like he believed it. He not only believed the words of the prophet Malachi, but he understood and embodied them in how he showed no partiality in the way he treated people. Booker was a master at fostering relationships because he knew his Master. Booker was owned by God, and

> There was a peace about Dr. Washington, which is evident in his writings and messages.

he respected men equally. There was a peace about Booker, which is evident in his writings and messages, that can be explained in no other way. Even those who opposed him respected him for the genuine respect and dignity he gave everyone.

Do we have common ground? Absolutely! It has been here since the beginning, and the Light continues to shine whether we allow it in our life or not. This is the vertical common ground that must be sought before we have any hope of finding horizontal common ground here on planet Earth.

Breath of God

My wife, Dianne, and I saw the movie *Jesus Revolution*, which is a true story of revival that broke out on the West Coast in the early 1970s and spread across the entire country. The hippies yearned for the same freedom expressed by Emma Lazarus, whose words are etched on the base of the Statue of Liberty. They found true freedom in Jesus Christ, through the ministry of Chuck Smith and

Lonnie Frisbee. If you haven't seen the movie, please do your heart a favor and see it. It will give you some insight into the reality of being delivered from the brokenness of this world and falling heart first into the kingdom of Christ. Emma Lazarus' words describe what is appealing about being a follower of Christ: "Give me your tired, your poor, your huddled masses yearning to breathe free."[2] Her words describe redemption—without redemption, there is no freedom; without freedom, there is no peace. Grace is coming to grips with just how broken you are, yet knowing you have a Savior who not only knows your sufferings but delivers you from it.

Booker internalized the words of Emma Lazarus, then set out to grab every opportunity that came his way in a time when nothing came easy to a Black man in a world controlled by Whites. However, on that tiny hill in rural Alabama, the tired and poor assembled in huddled masses, yearning to breathe free. While freedom remained a dream for most Black Americans, the aroma of freedom in the nostrils of the students and faculty inside the boundaries of Tuskegee gave hope for freedom yet to be manifested in the hearts of those who controlled the world outside of Tuskegee.

Words from the heart often speak a different narrative than words from the mind. What is habitually done in the mind becomes a stronghold in the heart. My mind may know the right thing to do, but my heart may not yet be in it. This is evident in the writings of the founding fathers, who created the Constitution and the Declaration of Independence. Some were owners of human property, yet they penned the words that would ultimately set free those who were in bondage when these documents were adopted.

Tuskegee remains the benchmark of freedom.

The words in the Constitution came from a collection of minds, all different yet all had their eye on the prize: freedom. A little over a hundred years after America declared her independence from the mother country, Booker T.

Washington founded Tuskegee Institute, the most vivid expression of the freedoms granted by the Constitution. Tuskegee remains the benchmark of freedom, even now over a hundred and fifty years later.

In my opinion, Booker T. Washington was "The Greatest American." Born a slave, overcoming injustice and oppression, ascending to the highest place of respect worldwide, he embodied the very essence of the freedoms the founders knew could only be granted by God. Booker once said, "I have learned that success is to be measured not so much by the position that one has reached in life as by the obstacles which he has overcome while trying to succeed."[3] He not only overcame obstacles, but he denied them, not by demanding but by serving.

> **He embodied the very essence of the freedoms the founders knew could only be granted by God.**

The world is difficult and divided today, but nowhere near what Booker T. Washington encountered in his life. It was no different for George Washington Carver, because it is impossible to mention one without the other as the greatest Americans. What allowed these two men to overcome the dark world around them resided in their kindred hearts. They remained steadfast, never allowing bitterness toward those who oppressed them to control them nor did they allow it to take root in their hearts

One of Dr. Washington's greatest addresses to his students came at the end of a school year. These encouraging words were no doubt inspirational to the students at Tuskegee. My hope is that they will be inspirational to you as well.

> We have come to the close of another school year. Some of you will go out from among us now, not to return. Others will go home for the summer

vacation and return at the end of that for the next school year.

As you go out, there is one thing that I want to especially caution you about. Don't go home and feel that you are better than the rest of the folks in your neighbourhood because you have been away at school. Don't go home and feel ashamed of your parents because you think they don't know as much as you think you know. Don't think that you are too good to help them. It would be better for you not to have any education, than for you to go home and feel ashamed of your parents, or not want to help them. . . .

Be polite; to white and coloured people, both. It is possible for you, by paying heed to this, to do a great deal toward securing and preserving pleasant relations between the people of both races in the South. Try to have your manners in this respect so good that people will notice them and ask where you have been, at what school you learned to be so polite. You will find that politeness counts for a great deal, not only in helping you to get work, but in helping you to keep it.

Don't be ashamed to go to church and Sunday school . . . Show that education has only deepened your interest in such things. Have no going backward. Be clean, in your person, your language and in your thoughts.

It seems appropriate during these closing days of the school year to re-emphasize, if possible, that for which the institution stands. We want to have every student get what we have—in our egotism, perhaps—called the "Tuskegee spirit"; that is, to get hold of the spirit of the institution, get hold of that for which it stands; and then spread that spirit just as widely as possible, and plant it just as deeply as it is possible to plant it.[4]

There are more opportunities for men and women of all colors today than were available to Washington and Carver. They gave us a template for success as a nation and peace in the hearts of our people, yet we failed to follow it. Our culture wants life without structure, diplomas without education, and entitlements with no investment of hard work. With no cultural ethic of personal responsibility, we have become focused on ourselves, which is the recipe for a miserable life.

> They gave us a template for success as a nation and peace in the hearts of our people.

We must love and trust like Booker if we truly desire a better world for our children and grandchildren. We can begin by telling others about the life and character of this great American. We must embrace the principles of grace, forgiveness, and dignity for all people. We must choose to see the best in people rather than the worst. We must choose to serve each other. We must allow the breath of God to fill our heart with His love and grace. Only then will we all truly be free.

> *Nobody can give us those qualities merely by praising us and talking well about us; and when we possess them, nobody can take them from us by speaking ill of us.*
> —Booker T. Washington

Heart to Heart

The physical human heart is an organ that weighs less than a pound and is bright red when fresh oxygen-filled blood flows in from the lungs. When the heart is drained of life-giving blood, it is white. As I thought about the irony in that, it occurred to me that God may be revealing a poignant yet gracious truth regarding the heart and its contents.

The analogy here is between our physical heart and the heart of our soul. If our human heart is white when it is devoid of blood, the same can be said of our soul's heart when it is devoid of the blood of Jesus. God could very well be giving us a powerful metaphor of the unimportance of our color on the outside versus the intangible truth regarding His color on the inside. God places no value on the color of our skin: it is irrelevant to the condition of our heart, which is what really matters.

> *For the Lord does not see as man sees;*
> *for man looks at the outward appearance,*
> *but the Lord looks at the heart.*
> —1 Samuel 16:7

What's in your heart? Is it slow to anger, or is it agitated or maybe just broken and sorrowful? Is the color of your heart white, filled with pride and prejudice, void of the life-giving blood of the Lamb? Or, by God's grace through the finished work of His Son and our Savior Jesus Christ, is it bright red? There's a simple answer to these very complex and difficult questions. His name is Jesus.

Booker T. Washington left us a template in Tuskegee that was radical, redemptive, and remedial. Unless we follow his example, we are leaving our children and grandchildren with a world that will not only remain confused and angry, but it will remain divided. We are a lost people, and without the love and mercy of God through the Son who sets us free, we have no hope. Our only hope is in Jesus, and when our heart is truly emancipated, we will be free at last.

The best and most beautiful things
in the world cannot be seen or even touched.
They must be felt with the heart.
—Helen Keller

Dignity

Booker T. Washington said, "No race can prosper till it learns that there is as much dignity in tilling a field as in writing a poem."[5] He knew well the difference between tilling a field and writing a poem because he had experienced both and was at peace in performing either task. Dignity was such an important component in how he related to and interacted with every person he encountered. It is like he participated in a relational co-op with God to do His will on earth as it is in heaven. By cooperating with God, Booker knew God's will and purpose for his life. He participated with God, as His representative for mankind, accepting the responsibility of stewarding an entire race, of founding and leading the men and women of Tuskegee, and of building the Tuskegee template of heaven on earth for people of all nations and all walks of life.

We don't talk much about dignity today. It's just a word for most of us, but the lack of dignity may cause someone to ask, "Why am I less than? Am I worthy?" There are a number of ways dignity can be experienced. First, dignity requires empathy to comprehend the meaning of expressing dignity for each person you come in contact with, but also being aware when dignity is being denied. How we treat others is a good barometer of our comprehension of dignity. It begins with our thoughts toward others, especially those who don't look like you.

An opportunity came my way to work on the set of *The Chosen.* My friend Tim Hogan was selected as the lead on-site artist for the items made of wood, like doors, windows, and Roman carvings. I jumped at the chance, hoping to be discovered by Dallas Jenkins as maybe a stand-in for Judas. Just kidding. The truth is, I wanted to hang out with Tim and make a few extra bucks. It was great being on the set and working with such a diverse group. Hogan's heroes consisted of Black, White, Hispanic, young, and old types working together to make something beautiful to bring glory to God on TV.

While our little group worked together, there were many more men and women actually building the set. It was a working environment where each person was essentially equal yet under the ultimate authority of God. There was, of course, a hierarchy of management roles, with us underlings interacting in our own group. But there was an environment of equality in the way the upper-tier people treated the worker bees. Engaging with and working among men and women who didn't look like me in a situation where everyone was equal opened my eyes to what Booker said regarding dignity. I was beginning to comprehend the meaning of dignity.

> I was beginning to comprehend the meaning of dignity.

Dignity has a much deeper meaning than we may think. Dignity means nobility, elevation of character, or worth. Worthy is the word that best describes dignity for me. What makes one worthy? Is it his job, how much money he makes, where he goes to church, the car he drives, or the toys he possesses? I don't think so.

Another of my part-time jobs is parking cars at Dickies Arena in Fort Worth. Much the same as my job with *The Chosen*, I did it to stay active and make a few bucks. At the same time, it was an opportunity to engage with people who don't look like me. I knew I would be working with people across many levels of social status. Little did I know I would get a larger education in the grace of dignity.

As a parking garage attendant, I stepped out of my world of being comfortably retired into the world of the working class. I had the privilege of experiencing how upper-class elites interact with people of a lower social status. I was one of them and was considered equal to the other workers in the eyes of those attending the rodeo, and to my surprise, there were many who engaged with my Black coworkers the same as they engaged with me—and I loved it. Then there were those who seemed almost offended when spoken to first. This was even true with Blacks and Hispanics. It was an interesting experience of people-watching. It is in my nature to talk to people, interact, even kid around, so I had a lot of fun with it. Some people smiled and engaged as though I was equal to them, which opened my eyes to how important it is to show dignity, regardless of skin color, job, or social status. Being created equally by God is what makes each one of us worthy of dignity.

> It opened my eyes to how important it is to show dignity to another person, regardless of skin color, job, or social status.

There is a larger education available to all of us when we pay attention. Noticing someone and offering a friendly smile acknowledges that they are not invisible. The more I thought about it, the more I realized the simple joy of being around people who don't think they are better than you. God revealed His expression of dignity in how we relate to each other as equals. Because the name of Jesus is worthy, we are all worthy in Him. There are no exceptions to this truth.

It comes easy for a man of great means to have an elevated opinion of himself when in the presence of a parking lot attendant. The same is true of a college upperclassman in the presence of a lowly freshman who just walked on campus, or a corporate CEO in the presence of the person who cleans the restrooms. We tend to do this subconsciously, and too often we never consider that a man with a broom is equal to you and me in the eyes of God. He may be invisible horizontally, but he is vividly visual to our Creator God. It glorifies our Father when we are aware of and consider that the other person has the same dignity in the eyes of God as do we. This is a huge blind spot for all of us, and until I experienced it firsthand, I must admit I had been guilty of being indifferent toward people who serve to make my life more pleasant. Think about going to the grocery store and finding what you came to buy. Someone stocked that shelf. When you go to QuikTrip or Buc-ee's, every single item has been placed by someone, and the restroom has been cleaned—and we never give a thought to express gratitude, a simple "thank you" to the person who provided our pleasant experience. This is dignity, and it requires awareness and intentionality.

There is dignity in the color of our skin as well, and it is a huge determiner in how we treat each other. You may be a White attorney or doctor, driving a Range Rover, living in a million-dollar home. It is human nature to allow such material wealth to elevate our opinion of ourselves. Counting our blessings is an effective way to keep our minds from overstating our importance in the world. Gratitude is a choice, and it's the foundation for a humble heart. It is a major challenge to remain humble when your possessions place you in an elite group or class. Earlier in the book I quoted Emmett Scott, Booker's executive secretary, and the quote bears repeating here: "The Tuskegee Idea always asks one question, and that is, 'What are you?' and not, 'What have you?' The man who does not rise superior to his possessions does not measure up to the Tuskegee idea of manhood."[6] It is as if there is a caste system determined by what we possess more than who we are. We are divided by income, by the car we drive, and by our career. Even where our children go to school may cause us to look down on someone because their child attends a public school. Booker was

> There is as much dignity in digging a ditch or parking a car as there is in writing a book or producing a podcast.

right regarding dignity, and to put his words in today's vernacular, there is as much dignity in digging a ditch or parking a car as there is in writing a book, producing a podcast, or serving as CEO of a major corporation.

There is dignity in whatever you do when you cast down your bucket where you are. Dignity is the outcome of showing appreciation for the tasks others do that make life better for you. Living in a constant state of awareness and seeing others as God sees them will open your heart to love as God loves and to dignify them, whether they are a janitor or a head of state. Each person is worthy of dignity because, like you, their value is not horizontal; it is vertical. Yes, they may be in a different place in the eyes of the world, but in the eyes of God, we are all the same in Christ Jesus.

The challenge is not allowing ourselves to get caught up in the ascension of self but to follow Booker's reality of dignity. To quote him again, "There is as much dignity in tilling a field as in writing a poem."[7] What a beautiful way to experience and express the beauty of God's grace in how we interact with each other.

People want to know that they matter. They need to know God loves them right where they are. God is love, and He put His love in us through the finished work of Jesus. "We love Him because He first loved us" (1 John 4:19).

The next time you are in Walmart, your favorite grocery store, or some other place where you shop, be aware of the person stocking shelves, the cashier, the greeter, or the guy or gal gathering the shopping carts. Make eye contact and say, "Thank you. What you do is important to everyone who walks through the front door. I just wanted you to know how much I appreciate how you serve." They may look at you like you have three heads, but then again, what you said could bring a heartfelt response, even a tear, simply to be noticed and appreciated. Booker was right about so much, but he was masterful when it came to the grace of dignity.

Harmonic Grace

Dr. Washington recognized the power of grace, the innocence in the heart of a child, and how to harmonize our differences.

When Christ was upon this earth He said: "A little child shall lead them." Whence comes this supreme power of leadership? In this age, when we hear so much said about leaders of men, about successful leadership, we do well to stop to consider this admonition of the Saviour. Some are said to lead in business, others in education, others in politics, or in religion. What is the explanation of "A little child shall lead them"? Simply this. A little child, under all circumstances, is its simple, pure, sweet self; never appearing big when it is little; never appearing learned when it is ignorant; never appearing wealthy when it is in poverty; never appearing important when it is unimportant. In a word, the life of the child is founded upon the great and immutable, and yet simple, tender and delicate laws of nature. There is no pretense. There is no mockery.

There is an unconscious, beautiful, strong clinging to truth; and it is this divine quality in child or in man, in Jew or Gentile, in Christian or Mohammedan, in the ancient world or in the modern world, in a black man or in a white man, that always has led men and moulded their activity. The men who have been brave enough, wise enough, simple enough, self-denying enough to plant themselves upon this rock of truth and there stand, have, in the end, drawn the world unto them, even as Christ said: "I will draw all men unto me." Such a man was Luther, such a man was Wesley, such a man was Carlyle, such a man was Cromwell, such were Garrison and Phillips, such was Abraham Lincoln, and such was our own great Frederick Douglass.

The thing aimed at by all great souls has been to bring men and races back to the simplicity and purity of childhood—back to reality.

What is the most original product with which the Negro race stands accredited? Yes, I am almost ready to add, with which America stands accredited? Without hesitation I answer:—Those beautiful, weird, quaint, sweet melodies which were the simple, child-like expression of the anguish, the joy, the hopes, the burdens, the faith, the trials of our forefathers who wore the yoke of slavery.

Why are they the admiration of the world? Why does every attempt at improvement spoil them? Why do they never fail to touch the tenderest chord—to bring tears from the eyes of rich and poor—from king and humblest toiler alike?[8]

The "beautiful, weird, quaint, sweet melodies" Booker referred to are the Negro spirituals. Most people do not know these beautiful spirituals are mostly played on the black keys of the piano. There are five black notes on the piano known as the pentatonic scale, also known as the slave scale. The Negro spirituals were written on those five notes.

There are also white spirituals composed by white musicians on the slave scale. The most famous of the white spirituals is "Amazing Grace," written by John Newton, who was the captain of a slave ship. Many believe that Newton heard

> There is no harmony until the black keys are played with the white keys.

the melody for "Amazing Grace" from the belly of the ship where the slaves were held in chains. The melody sounds like a West African sorrow chant, and when Newton heard the melody, he penned the words to the song. There is no harmony until the black keys are played with the white keys. The same is true with people. Relational harmony happens when we enter the divide with a spiritual blend of mercy and grace, which is truly amazing.

The beauty of the harmony when the black keys and the white keys are played together is by design. We, too, are designed to be played together, by the Master Composer, on the piano of life. God designed us to live life together in harmonious community with Christ, where Black meets White, high meets low, the native-born meets the immigrant, and the Northern Yankee meets the Southern redneck. When love and grace are the theme, the lives of Christians together becomes God's melody of harmonic grace.

Tune my heart to sing Thy grace.
—Robert Robinson, "Come, Thou Fount of Every Blessing"

Walk a Mile in My Shoes

"First of all," he said, "if you can learn a simple trick, Scout, you'll get along a lot better with all kinds of folks. You never really understand a person until you consider things from his point of view—until you climb into his skin and walk around in it."[9]

These words were spoken by Atticus Finch to his daughter, Scout, in *To Kill a Mockingbird*, and they are the essence of the challenge we all face in comprehending each other, respecting our differences, and placing high value on what we have in common.

Over the years, I have had many friends of color. I knew them growing up, attended school together, played on sports teams, even went to church together, but I never really *knew* them. I don't recall having any misgivings about getting to know them; I just never thought about it. I'm not really certain why this was the case, but more than likely it was because we hung out in separate worlds: them in their world of Black friends and me in my world of White friends. We never had issues but never intentionally engaged each other either. We simply never considered entering the divide between our worlds. It was an unintentional indifference that none of us recognized. I believe that indifference remains today among all races, and we never give thought to it. Hmm, I think that may define indifference.

> We simply never considered entering the divide between our worlds.

We do something similar today in that we pass each other on the street, maybe work together, but never have a real conversation over lunch or a cup of coffee. Even at church, we smile and nod as we pass each other in the aisles of our sanctuaries, even sit next to each other in worship, yet never care enough to know that person who doesn't look like us on a more personal level. This is indifference, and I am speaking to everyone here, all of us. We tend to stick to our comfort zone, if you know what I mean. We are indifferent to the invisible chasm or divide that separates us, and unless we choose to enter that divide, we will never know who that person is or that they could possibly become a really good friend. It is in the center of this divide that we meet the person who draws us together—Jesus. He is the place where we will discover the beauty of relational grace and friendship on a deeper level. Grace is never indifferent.

Until God planted the seed that has sprouted into the calling to write this book, I was indifferent—or maybe ignorant is a better description. Remember what you read earlier regarding my journey to Tuskegee? That journey has led me to new friendships that are more than simple acquaintances. I have friends now who have opened an entirely new world of enlightenment, and I am blessed beyond measure.

Once I entered the divide, God opened my eyes to the reality of life from someone else's point of view, and it has been humbling, to say the least. It has also revealed what I have missed by not having friends of color. There is a different dynamic in friendships when people who don't look like each other leave their comfort zones and enter the divide. God reveals a deeper and richer comprehension of His grace in our orbit of friendships. Opening our hearts to one another and sharing our stories allows us to experience a revelation of grace like never before.

> God reveals a deeper and richer comprehension of His grace in our orbit of friendships.

I would never know these amazing stories had I not gone deeper into the reality of those willing to share their experiences as a person who is not White. I never realized the pain of being born with a stigma that culture defines as "less than." I know that now, only because of what I have learned from those who invited me into their reality. It is a reality I want to share with everyone, because it is by and for grace that we enter the divide. This is centric in comprehending God's definition of grace and how it permeates the fabric of our lives.

Grace is being forgiven for my sins and then forgiving those in my life for the sins committed against me and against those whom I value. Grace is also forgiving myself for the sins I know I committed against God and His children, including me. "For all have sinned and fall short of the glory of God" (Romans 3:23). God created us all in His image; He made us equals. Man has figured out a way to elevate himself, one race above another. Only God, in His grace, can bring us back to the bedrock of being one race, one color, in His kingdom. This is critical to comprehending grace and then interpreting it, with the love of our Savior, to others.

CHAPTER TEN

Grace of Thick Skin

Choosing to be unoffendable, or relinquishing my right to anger, does not mean accepting Injustice. It means actively seeking justice, and loving mercy, while walking humbly with God. And that means remembering I'm not Him. What a relief.
—Brant Hansen

Becoming Unoffendable

To get offended and to offend others are facts of life we all experience. Whether we stay offended or not is determined by the strength of our faith. To remain offended, allowing the stronghold of bitterness to take root in our heart, is the choice we make if our faith is week. To get over it and move on is what Jesus did, and obviously, there was no one with a stronger faith than our Lord. He was often offended, but He always turned the other cheek, never retaliating for sins against Him nor did He harbor bitterness toward sinners. Jesus never allowed it to change how He responded and how He treated someone. When He cleared the temple of the merchants, it was definitely a moment of righteous anger, but He never said anything like, "I can't believe you guys" or "I was hurt deeply by what you did." He never shamed anyone, except maybe the Pharisees because of their self-righteousness. If you go to any of the Gospels and read the stories of Jesus encountering a person living in sin, He simply forgave them and told them to go and sin no more. On the cross He petitioned God, "Father, forgive them, for they do not know what they do" (Luke 23:34). In short, Jesus was unoffendable.

As I thought about the word *unoffendable*, I went online to Dictionary.com for a definition. It's not there. The word *offend* is, but *unoffendable* must not be considered a word. However, when I googled it, I discovered a link to a book, *Unoffendable*, written by West Coast talk-show host Brant Hansen. *Unoffendable* carries the heart-emancipating message that to be offended is a given, but to remain offended is a choice. The outcome is learning to steward your anger caused by words or actions of another and to release the drama in the moment of being offended. It actually sounds absurd, but when you think about it, it makes sense because people are going to continue to offend us. Like Jesus, you can actually live in a perpetual state of forgiveness. You never have to allow the things people do and say to steal your joy. At the very least, when you forgive the offenses of others in advance, you can lower the temperature of how you respond.

In Matthew, Jesus said, "For if you forgive men their trespasses, your heavenly Father will also forgive you. But if you do not forgive men their trespasses, neither will your Father forgive your trespasses" (Matthew 6:14-15). Sin is referred to here as a trespass, but I believe a trespass can also qualify as an offense or anything someone does or says by bullying their way into our space, either physically or emotionally. We have a choice whether to remain offended or not. We can get pissed off and pooch our lips out like a narrow-mouthed frog, or we can choose to stay calm, show a little maturity, and respond graciously because we have chosen to live with a forgiving spirit. When we plan ahead to forgive, the offenses roll like water off a duck's back. Forgiving ahead of time is what Jesus did, and people smarter than me call this "prevenient grace." Prevenient grace is living with a spirit of forgiveness for the offenses that are to come.

Jesus initiated the idea of prevenient grace when He petitioned God, from the cross, to "forgive them, for they do not know what they do" (Luke 23:34). Jesus forgave "them"—including you and me—for their sins in advance. He knew beforehand what sins were going to be committed and who was going to commit them, and He had forgiven them prior to the offense. He knows your sins as well as mine and has forgiven them all, not just those in the past but the ones we are committing today, and the ones we will commit for the rest of our lives on planet Earth. By God's grace, you and I can choose to live the same way, in a perpetual state of forgiving our offenders.

You learn to overlook petty offenses, or even the significant ones.

That doesn't mean you will never get offended, but what it does mean is you will be quick to forgive and move on like Jesus, over and over. Plus, you develop thick skin. You learn to overlook petty offenses, or even the significant ones. As you grow spiritually, the choices you make to be unoffendable will be liberating. Brant Hansen said it well in *Unoffendable*: "Ministry itself, serving others, has to involve deciding not to be offended."[1]

Booker T. Washington was unoffendable, and his emancipated heart was the outcome of his paradigm shift from seeing the world as a Black man to seeing the world through the eyes of His resurrected Lord. He knew that the Spirit that raised Jesus from the dead was the same Spirit that resurrected his life from the bondage of slavery. Booker was certainly more than an emancipated slave. He experienced true freedom when he surrendered his will to God, who set him free to live, love, and serve mankind of all nations. Booker never allowed the offenses and mistreatment of ignorant White people to keep him from being successful. He remained steadfast to his calling and purpose by choosing to have thick skin.

Think about how much more stable your emotional health and your relationships would be if you worked at becoming unoffendable, or at least made an effort to keep bitterness from taking root. By nature, people do and say things that are offensive. When we leave the offenses of others at the foot of the cross, we can actually become unoffendable. This battle rages in the mind, but with practice and the help of the Holy Spirit, your heart can certainly be transformed to the likeness of Christ. You can choose to be unoffendable.

One of the greatest gifts we can give our kids is to help them learn not to take themselves too seriously and instead to develop thick skin. When we learn to take ourselves less seriously and not internalize things that are said to us or about us, it is liberating. You may disagree if you are highly sensitive and easily offended. I know guys who are big and strong, but you can't kid around with them because they get offended. It's almost like there's a child in the body of an adult. Walking around on eggshells because someone is oversensitive and self-conscious is no fun, so strengthen your friendships by becoming unoffendable. People will enjoy your company more as you lighten up and refuse to be the victim of the things people say and do.

> **We experience the freedom to be ourselves.**

Think about how much better we would get along with our spouse if we held our tongue from any need to correct or impose our vast knowledge of whatever is happening in the moment. To sit down and listen instead of expressing meaningless rhetoric that adds nothing but tension is certainly more in line with how Jesus engaged with others. The same is true with our kids. It is okay to speak up; it is not okay to have a need to speak up. Ouch! I think I just offended myself with that last sentence.

> **It is okay to speak up; it is not okay to have a need to speak up.**

Now is a good time to do a little self-evaluation. This is where we consider the possibility that we may be living as a victim in a perpetual state of offendability. When we hear things that are true, yet uncomfortable and hard to hear, we initially become offended. When these new truths take root in our heart, our mind can then begin to release whatever hang-ups we may have, even bitterness, that keep us from being easier to live and work with. I never said this would be easy, but getting down to the bottom—the bedrock and foundation of the stronghold in our embittered heart—is where healing takes place.

When we become followers of Jesus, we enter the race for grace in its most glorious expression. When we are authentic in knowing and being known by God, His grace and mercy are manifested in us. When this happens, we live with a forgiving heart that is free and unoffendable. For sure, people—even those closest to us whom we love and who love us—will continue to do and say things that irritate and offend us. Plus, there are some people in the world who are just mean. The key to victory is the quick release of the impulse to be offended. The outcome of being unoffendable is peace.

> *How much easier and simpler it is to meet prejudice*
> *with sympathy and understanding than with hatred . . .*
> *if you simply refuse to feel injured by what he says.*
> —Booker T. Washington

Labels

We have become a culture of accusers that weaponize the use of labels to describe another person or group based on unfounded assumptions. Labels have become so overused that, over time, they begin to lose their power and intended purpose. When we label someone, we become judge and jury, saying, "I know who you are; you ain't foolin' me."

Perhaps the most overused and falsely applied label we hear today is "racist." Playing the race card has become the most effective way to delegitimize someone you disagree with politically or otherwise because mainstream media, more often than not, repeats the labeling, regardless of whether or it is true. The goal for the accuser is to minimize and cancel the other person from having influence on what the public believes, and it works in a culture with little regard for truth. People get called a racist because of something that has absolutely nothing to do with skin color. However, it is an easy way for people who have no real foundation for the label they apply to expose their lack of knowledge by bullying and demeaning the person who, in most cases, makes more sense. We live in fear of being called racist—so much so, that we refuse to disagree with someone who doesn't look like us. Labels are damaging, especially when they are misused and simply untrue. But that doesn't stop evil people from using them. Lying is the native tongue of the devil and his colleagues, which the media, all too often, agrees with.

The label that grieves me the most is "Uncle Tom." Booker T. Washington was most often criticized by his own people. He was a man of knowledge, integrity, wisdom, character, and he had a heart for mankind regardless of the color of their skin. Because he led with selflessness and independence, and chose not to lead with entitlement and the condemnation of White people, he was criticized. The same is true today as many men and women of the Black race are labeled "Uncle Tom."

If you have read *Uncle Tom's Cabin*, you know where this label comes from. Tom was a slave, a Black man who had moved beyond bitterness as a slave and was actually free inside while in bondage on the outside. Tom lived among and cooperated with Whites and served them in a loving and merciful way. Booker would say, "Tom cast down his bucket where he was." Because Tom lived and operated in the White man's world without malice, his name is used by the true racists to belittle and delegitimize successful Blacks who have grown and matured beyond bitterness to a life of serving America and her people. The beauty of Uncle Tom's heart was that he was not a slave unto himself. Tom was emancipated from the inside out, from the bondage of bitterness, and found peace and true freedom. He understood ownership and being personally responsible versus depending on someone else to provide for his needs. Tom was no longer a victim; he had become a victor and was unoffendable. When I hear a Black man or woman labeled "Uncle Tom," I know they are a successful person of knowledge and noble character. It is ironic that a Black person who labels another Black "Uncle Tom" is bestowing the highest compliment on their target while convicting themselves of being the opposite.

Some of the men and women who've been given the "Uncle Tom" label are Dr. Ben Carson, Larry Elder, Candace Owens, Thomas Sowell, Lieutenant Colonel Allen West, Dr. Carol Swain, Shelby Steele, and Robert Woodson. Every one of these men and women have something in common. They are successful, and they all have minds that have been emancipated from the root of bitterness. They know their true identity does not flow out of their Blackness but out of their likeness to Christ. Like Booker, they are unoffendable.

Christian Nationalism is a relatively new term that is being thrown around in culture today by people who are neither Christian nor National. The goal for this label is to describe men and women who love God and country as dangerous and a threat to democracy. Nothing could be further from the truth. When you look deeper into what is driving this false narrative, the label is born out of disdain for our founders and the brilliance of the Constitution. The Constitution limits power, and it drives them nuts that the founders were wise enough to set limits on the government by empowering "we the people." To fear God and love Jesus, to value family and love country, and to be law-abiding is antithetical to who they are. These egotistical elites hate America; they hate that her founding fathers were Christian; and their desire is to destroy anyone in America who lives under the authority of King Jesus. These types are the true threat to democracy. Booker said, "Egotism is the anesthetic that dulls the pain of stupidity."[2] There is no better description of people who disagree simply because their hunger for power is greater than their love for their country under the authority of God.

Definitions belong to the definers, not the defined.
—Toni Morrison, Beloved

Guilt

Confessing guilt is like a two-sided coin—on one side is the admission of offending or sinning against another human being, and on the other side is how the confession is received. This sets in motion a process of mercy or condemnation. Confessed guilt either empowers the offended and provides cause for aggression (often passive), or gives an opportunity for the offended to honor the words of Jesus when He said, "My yoke is easy and My burden is light" (Matthew 11:30), releasing the burden of guilt that is a heavy weight to bear. Believing the words of Jesus is the key to forgiving and moving on, placing a higher value on relationship with the offender than power over the offender.

It's important to remember, confession of an offense is trusting that knowledge with the offended party. The offender is humbling themselves before the offended and asking for mercy. One may feel that mercy is not deserved, but none of us deserves God's mercy. He willingly gives us this undeserved mercy every moment of every day. This is grace, and it is vital to living life free and clear of the bitterness that robs our joy.

Confessed guilt transfers the power of knowledge from the confessor to the offended. The challenge for the oppressed is whether to steward this power for restoring the relationship or exploiting it for reasons rooted in selfishness.

It is not unlike when a husband confesses that he broke his marriage vows and committed the sin of adultery. The wife has a choice to make. If she chooses to forgive and reconcile, her challenge going forward is not to use her husband's confessed guilt against him, holding it over his head for the remainder of their marriage when things don't go her way. Or if she truly forgives him and has mercy on him, restoring trust in her husband, she will not hold the affair over her husband's head for the purpose of manipulating him. Restoring trust is key to ongoing peace in any relationship, and this especially applies to racial reconciliation.

In one way or another, guilt and mercy play out in our lives every day. Maintaining relationships is hard, even with those rare individuals considered kindhearted and gracious. This has never been truer than in our relationships with those who don't look like us. We are all guilty of prejudicial thoughts and behavior, whether we realize it or not. The color of our skin or our ethnicity has been a weapon of the devil to divide God's children since Adam and Eve were lied to in the Garden of Eden. The sad thing is how little we talk about this tactic of the enemy of God with those who don't look like us. Until we can set aside our differences—starting with the color of our skin—we will never call it for what it is. It is the evil that came to steal, kill, and destroy, and he has certainly done that in America, dividing us based on the color of our skin. He has done this cunningly by creating an unconscious prejudice regarding those who don't look like us.

The two-sided coin also reflects racial division. In his book *White Guilt: How Blacks and Whites Together Destroyed the Promise of the Civil Rights Era*, Shelby Steele explored the whole idea of guilt and its power over peace in our relationships. Steele wrote about civil rights becoming the center of attention when President Johnson signed the Civil Rights Bill into law in 1964. This

For the first time in history, Whites began to own their past sins of oppression and injustice on a large scale.

was the beginning of the end of White supremacy and created a phenomenon in the minds of White liberals that Steele identified as "white guilt." As I read *White Guilt*, the truth of how and why

Americans are so divided by race came more into focus. When White people in the sixties became aware of how their race had treated people of the Black race, and no doubt other races as well, the weight of guilt was heavy. For the first time in history, Whites began to own their past sins of enslaving humans, oppression, and injustice on a large scale. Sadly, there are Whites who still believe in the supremacy of people with White skin. However, in this book we are going to focus on those who were willing to own their part in the mistreatment of others.

As White people acknowledged and took ownership of our historical and generational sins, the Blacks became empowered like never before. The idea of White guilt was new to me until I read Steele's book, and that is when the rush to social justice after the death of George Floyd made total sense. I didn't get it at the time, but now I totally get why churches moved so quickly to embrace the Black Lives Matter (BLM) ideology, even participating in BLM marches and rallies. They fell victim to believing they were guilty simply because they were White. If they chose not to participate in the events ordained and promoted by the race-baiters, they risked being identified as racist—and no one wants to be called a racist, especially if you are White. That is what happens when we forget where we came from and fail to pass the truth of our historical past to the following generations.

I was invited to march in a BLM march, and I declined—but not because I don't believe that Black lives matter. I declined because something just didn't feel right about how the church was rushing to join a cultural narrative versus the Christ-centeredness of the love of God. I had questions that I couldn't answer. I couldn't understand how a church that historically welcomed people of all races had suddenly agreed with culture instead of leading with her true identity as the body of Christ.

In *White Guilt*, Shelby Steele described the power of White guilt and how it was mis-stewarded on both sides of the racial divide. It is White guilt that created anxiety in many church leaders and led them to adopt woke ideologies that are contagious and destructive, doing nothing to provide solutions. We all share the cause and effect of this guilt. There is always a victim when an offense is committed. When we are a victim of the sin of others, we have a choice. Either we remain in the state of victimhood, allowing ourselves to fall into the trap that leads to becoming a bitter victim, or we refuse to participate.

If you are Black, what you do with the knowledge of the oppression against you and your race is essential to lighten the burden of bitterness toward your White neighbors. It is time to bring an end to the divide between races, and that means we need to stop listening to the race-baiters that dominate mainstream media. We are all weary of the constant barrage from those who choose to hold power, and even make a living, based on the status of victimhood. But there is hope in the remnant of God's children whose hearts are full of grace and mercy rather than condemnation. Are you one of those in the remnant of mercy givers, or do you remain in bondage to the generational sin of condemning people simply because they are White? This is the kind of truth you more than likely will not hear from a pulpit. White pastors are especially cautious of saying anything that may feel offensive to their members who are Black. Notice I said *feel*. What feels offensive doesn't mean it actually is offensive. If you are Black, and that last sentence or two offends you, I hope you are graciously offended. The truth that sets us free can also piss us off until we come to grips with grace. It is by grace you will be set free.

> Confessed guilt in the hands of someone with weak faith can be a recipe for oppression rooted in self-righteousness and the temptation to gossip.

If you are White, do you live in shame because you think you are obligated to remain in a state of guilt? Please know that those sins of slavery and oppression were paid for on the cross, so you and I can live together in harmony with our friends who don't look like us. We're a confused people, and it is only by grace that we will discover freedom from ourselves. Shelby Steele put into perspective an accurate account of what Americans of both races have experienced over the past fifty years:

> I would argue that white guilt—this unforeseen diminution of moral authority that came after the open acknowledgment of racial wrongdoing—was a far more powerful force and commonly assumed. This is so because it replaced one of the greatest sources of moral authority in the history of the modern world: white supremacy.
>
> This was the authority that had given white America the hubris to live rather easily with slavery and segregation even as these practices glaringly violated every principle the nation was founded on. White supremacy—commonly accepted as a moral truth about the world, as a fact of nature reflecting God's intended hierarchy of races gave whites the moral authority to exclude other races from the American democracy as inferior. . . . The racist says, "My God-given authority is my authority, so my authority of inferiors is in God's plan. What I think is conclusive, and what I say determines the course of things because God and nature want it so." Nazis acted against Jews on the authority of their God-given Aryan superiority. Whites segregated blacks in America on the authority of God's gift to them of superiority. When America admitted racial wrongdoing and passed strong civil rights legislation in the 60's, it delegitimized exactly

this kind of authority—authority justified by an assertion that God made your group superior to all others.[3]

Steele hit the nail on the head describing how our opinion of ourselves overpowers the self-evident truth of what God says about us, individually and collectively. I do not know Mr. Steele, but I assume he is a man that believes in God and His moral authority.

Blacks who embrace the principles of forgiveness, grace, and personal responsibility continue to have success in America. Booker set the standard for this ideology of truth and sound judgment. He understood this early on and lived his life serving instead of demanding. He acknowledged the opportunities afforded to him in the Emancipation Proclamation and proceeded to make himself useful by building on every opportunity that came his way.

The Black race has more power today than ever before.

While the idea of government-funded welfare came from FDR, President Lyndon Johnson is responsible for signing the Civil Rights Bill into law in 1964, which has held the poor of all races in economic slavery. America became not just the provider of welfare but an enabler, removing any responsibility for their own well-being. The outcome has been keeping Blacks and poor Whites in bondage to dependence on the government for their very existence. We totally blew it by allowing this to happen and missing the opportunity to do what is best for the family long term—providing a lifeline to dignity as a self-supporting citizen. Instead, the Democrat party led the way in enabling the poor of both races to remain at the bottom rung of the economic ladder in America. This is how the Democrat party differs from the Republican party. Frederick Douglass, Booker T. Washington, and Abraham Lincoln were all Republicans in favor of self-reliance for all people. The Democrats favor government dependency, which transfers power from the people to the government.

After Johnson signed the Civil Rights Act of 1964, he stated in the Commencement Address at Howard University, "You do not take a person who, for years, has been hobbled by chains and liberate him, bringing him up to the starting line of a race and then say, 'you are free to compete with all the others.' . . . Equal opportunity is essential, but not enough."[4]

In an interview on *Uncommon Knowledge*, Steele said that Johnson's statement was a horrible historic mistake, saying, "We oppressed you, and now we are going to lift you up and redeem you. Your fate is in our hands. You don't see your fate as in your hands."[5] Oppression was philosophically transferred from "ruling over" to "being dependent on."

What President Johnson should have said is this: "You are now free to be your best and live according to God's purpose for your life. America will no longer stand in your way but will provide every means possible to help you carve out a life of respect, of individual responsibility, as a citizen of America. We will be better, and together we will become one nation under God." He should have empowered the beneficiaries of the Civil Rights Act rather than using it as a means of maintaining dominance.

> We allowed this to happen by missing the opportunity to raise up the man farthest down.

There were exceptions who didn't believe the lies of the party of slavery. Men like Shelby Steele, Lieutenant Colonel Allen West, and Ben Carson didn't believe it and worked their way to a successful life. Women like Carol Swain, Candace Owens, and Winsome Earle-Sears didn't believe the lies either. Booker would never have allowed the guilt harvesters to have so much power in his America. Yet, if he were here today, he would be vilified by Washington elites and the media.

Immediate gratification was inferior to Booker's ideology of equality of opportunity and drew fire from the race-baiters. Affirmative action will never fill the void in the hearts of Black Americans. Only by the grace of God will the afflictions in the hearts of men and women be healed. No one is going to do it for you, and no one is going to do it for me. It is together that we will find rest. Until we begin to live like we believe the solution is in our hearts, we will remain in slavery to the enemy of God.

Confession of guilt is the beginning of restoring peace. Mercy for the sinner and restoring peace are the next steps. Restoring racial harmony is only possibility until together we turn that possibility into reality. This is Washington's Tuskegee template in action.

Reparations

If you were to give reparations to everyone whose ancestors had been slaves, I suspect that you would have to give reparations to more than half the entire population of the globe. Slavery was not confined to one set of races.
—Thomas Sowell

It was a lunch gathering, and we were in a conversation about social justice when I made a comment about how I may have been accepted into college because I was privileged and not because of merit. I went on to say that if I had high test scores and high character but was Black, I may not have been accepted. Hopefully, that was not the case, but it certainly was something to consider.

That's when one of the guys made the comment, "That's why reparations make sense." When I heard those words, I realized how far we have moved from the reality of the Gospel of Jesus Christ. The truth is, Jesus paid reparations for the sins of all of us, even those ancestors who looked like me.

When we demand to be reimbursed for being sinned against, we are holding others liable for sins that Jesus forgave and justified on the cross. This truth includes the horrific historical sins of an entire race against another. I have no doubt this truth makes many of us uncomfortable. I will repeat another truth: "the truth will set you free" (John 8:32, NIV), but first it may make you uncomfortably angry. This truth will either divide us and keep us at odds with each other or it will set us free from holding each other liable for sins justified by our Lord to live in harmony with each other. You either believe what is true about the gospel of Jesus Christ or you do not. This is a very simple truth yet one we seldom hear from American pulpits because it offends many of our brothers and sisters who are Black, yet is critical to living according to the will of God and not our own.

In Ephesians 4:15, the apostle Paul writes. "Speak the truth in love." The following words by Paul David Tripp expose the truth in Paul's command.

> The call is to do theology in loving community with other people. Truth not spoken in love ceases to be true because it's bent and twisted by other human agendas. I cannot forsake truth for relationships, and I cannot forsake relationships for truth. They need to be held together, because we need to understand truth in community with one another to compensate for our blindness and bias, and we need truth to define for us what kind of community we should live in together.[6]

It is the battle we face every day, and that battle takes place in our mind. God is either the authority and has the final word in our lives or we live according to our own authority. If we believe in Him and who He is, we live each day to serve Him through the finished work of Jesus Christ or we live denying who He is and the truth that

He died for the forgiveness of my sins and for my sins against others. Jesus paid all our debts owed to each other so we can live in harmony.

Many of us believe that if we attend church on a regular basis, we have all we need to live life as a good man or woman in an uncivilized world. People walk through the doors of our churches every Sunday, broken from the sufferings of life, and leave without any hope of a better tomorrow. It seems the messages we hear in our churches are good but too often stop short of taking us to the truth of what keeps us in bondage to ourselves. This is especially true of messages that speak to the stronghold of anger and bitterness. "Perfect love casts out fear" (1 John 4:18) and that includes fear of speaking the truth regarding generational bitterness and anger among our Black brothers and sisters. This is a good example of the "no-go" zone where pastors stop short for fear of offending our friends who are Black. If we consider them friends and we desire to spend eternity with our friends, shouldn't we be telling the truth and nothing but the truth? Generational bitterness is sin just like all other sins and if we love, we must tell it like it is. I believe the Almighty will hold us accountable when we stop short for fear of offending those who need to hear the truth. Coming to grips with what keeps us in bondage to bitterness is essential to living free from yourself, whether you live to condemn one person or an entire race. Remember the words of the apostle in John 3:17, "For God did not send His son into the world to condemn the world, but to save the world through Him." If God didn't send Jesus into the world to condemn people, I doubt He expects you and me to condemn people either. I have a friend who is a former pastor, attorney, and family counselor who puts words to the bedrock truth of God's mystery of reconciliation.

These are the words of Jim Reynolds Sr. "I do not think the suggestion of reparations is necessarily an example of bitterness but a reach for justice; an effort at 'setting things right.'" Forgiveness, reconciliation, and justice are not mutually exclusive. The person who brought up reparations might have just been saying, "We have thrown black folks in a deep hole, and this might be a way to get them out." I do not advocate reparations because I have no idea how that might affect justice, but I do think the Church, generally, does not get justice or reconciliation.

As a Church, we do not understand that there should not be White and Black churches any more than there should have been Jewish and Gentile churches in Paul's day. Paul labored his whole life to administer the Mystery of oneness (Ephesians 2–4). Most churches that I know anything about are theologically and spiritually comatose when it comes to replicating now the "mystery" of reconciliation—one new humanity in Christ (Ephesians, Galatians, Colossians. etc.).

What concerns me is the continuing failure of the Church to apply reconciliation and justice as Disciples of Jesus—not as political activists. Churches are practicing a de facto segregation or what might be called a token integration right now. Neither White nor Black churches want to become one or even see why that might be God's will."

Jim and Donna Reynolds recently started and now lead a home church that is largely made up of poor African Americans—formerly citizens of West African nations, etc., now citizens who have migrated to the U.S. over the last twenty years. Jim has become their advocate to insurance companies, district attorneys, and landlords who take advantage of their naivete. Jim became aware of this through the home church small community where he hears their stories. They work long hours and are lovely people with not a thread of bitterness. Jim is their advocate because he follows Jesus. Jim loves Jesus and is a Disciple of Jesus and not progressive or conservative. He does not fit in any of the partisan camps, and he also advocates for justice for his Anglo, Hispanic, and Asian brothers and sisters.

Jim lives the narrative "to raise up the man farthest down." He has helped countless men and women who have come to trust him. They see beyond the color of his skin to the heart of Jesus that dwells inside. It's all part of the mystery of reconciliation that is critical to seeing as God sees. Each one of us has opportunities to do the same. There are many men and women available to help those who could use an advocate and a hand up for a better life. While they may have skin of different colors, they will have one thing in common: the heart of Jesus. Speaking truth in love and forgiveness is a message every one of us. Forgiveness is essential to the process of reconciliation and justice. We all are naive when it comes to the reality of the mystery of the gospel of a God who would walk among us interpreting Himself, then choose to die to set us free from ourselves. He is our advocate, and His name is Jesus.

If you would like to hear more from Jim Reynolds, tune into his podcast, *The Politics of Jesus*.

> *I do not set aside the grace of God,*
> *for if righteousness could be gained through the law,*
> *Christ died for nothing!*
> —Galatians 2:21 (NIV)

CHAPTER ELEVEN

Destination Grace

*Tomorrow's destiny becomes
today's direction.*
—John Maxwell

"Sir, why did you become interested in the school?"
. . .
 "It was because I felt even as a young man that
your people were somehow closely connected with
my destiny. Do you understand?"[1]

This conversation between a young Black student and a White philanthropist takes place in Ralph Ellison's classic novel *Invisible Man.* The "Do you understand?" question has been a recurring question for me throughout the writing of *Critical Grace.*

I received a call from a good friend regarding something our senior pastor said. Our pastor reminded us that the church had made a commitment to become at least twenty percent multiethnic in five years. The good news is we have surpassed that goal in less time. My friend, who happens to be White, was incensed and had a problem with the idea of the church having a goal of becoming a more multiethnic body of Christ. His misgivings were not motivated by the church becoming more diverse. His pushback came more from the numbers game too many churches get trapped into, especially megachurches.

Our church has historically been and remains a warm environment for all people of every race and every nation. I also think our church is no different from most historically White congregations in that we have remained in a state of unconscious segregation. I'm not saying that White churches are opposed to a diverse body of believers; we just don't think about actually entering the divide where hearts are integrated. The following Scripture reveals the will of God for His children.

> After these things I looked, and behold, a great multitude which no one could number, of all nations, tribes, peoples, and tongues, standing before the throne and before the Lamb, clothed with white robes, with palm branches in their hands, and crying out with a loud voice, saying, "Salvation belongs to our God who sits on the throne, and to the Lamb!" All the angels stood around the throne and the elders and the four living creatures, and fell on their faces before the throne and worshiped God, saying:
>
> "Amen! Blessing and glory and wisdom,
> Thanksgiving and honor and power and might,
> Be to our God forever and ever.
> Amen." (Revelation 7:9-12)

As I finished reading Revelation chapter 7, I read again the above passage and asked myself a couple of questions. First, I asked, "Is the apostle John prophesying what the church will look like when we stand before God as He sits on the throne?" If the answer is yes, my second question is in regard to how Jesus said we should pray in Matthew 6. Jesus instructed the apostles to pray like this: "Your kingdom come. Your will be done. On earth as it is in heaven" (Matthew 6:10). If the will of God is to be done "on earth as it is in heaven," should the church not look like the multitude described in Revelation 7? Imagine having a drone's view of what this multitude will look like. The image I envision is one like Joseph's coat of many colors or maybe the medicine wheel on the cover of this book.

When we cross the boundary of our differences into the divide between races, God opens the door and reveals a deeper comprehension and a more accurate interpretation of His redeeming grace. God never does anything based on race. He does everything according to His grace and the power of our resurrected Lord. When we confess Jesus as Lord and Savior, our destiny has been set. We will stand before the throne of God with our brothers and sisters who don't look like us, all nations, tribes, peoples, and tongues. It is up to us to allow God to magnify Himself in our hearts individually and collectively as the multiethnic body of Christ on earth as it is in heaven.

> **Your destiny is not determined by what you do, but in what God does through you.**

It would be easy to judge the nature of my friend's call as "racist." However, when you get down to bedrock, to his heartfelt concern, it had more to do with the church pursuing the appearance of diversity rather than the authenticity of real integration. We can integrate physically, but until our hearts are integrated with the heart of God, we will never have peace in our differences. It is all grace, and it is critical.

Process

Coach Nick Saban is known for his references to "process" in building a football team and the development of each player, individually. Each player is somewhere in the process of becoming the skilled football player Coach Saban envisions he can become. Who each young man becomes as a player determines whether he will earn a starting position on the team. While Coach Saban and his assistants observe and evaluate each player, they also pay attention to their development on the inside.

Life is very similar in that it's a process for each one of us. Within our life process, there are other processes that determine who we are becoming. Writing this book has been a process for me and is now an essential component to who I am becoming. Only you can interpret what your life process looks like. Who you are becoming is determined by where you are in your process; this becomes your story. Who you are becoming determines the legacy you will leave. The question we must all answer, whether we ask it or not, is "Will I leave a legacy of kindness, or will I leave the generations that follow a legacy of anger and hate?"

How we interpret guilt is a process. In my Tuskegee journey, I discovered three words that I knew but had never delved into the deeper comprehensions of their power. "Lament, Repent, and Implement" is the process of coming to grips with the sins we have committed against God and others. This is also the process of forgiving the sins others have committed against us personally, and collectively as a race or ethnicity. The process of forgiveness is an acquired taste, and the flavor gets a little sweeter with each bite. I love the way Paul David Tripp described the process of a life being transformed to the likeness of Jesus: "God's work in you is a process, not an event. It progresses not in three or four huge moments, but in ten thousand little moments of change. . . . Personal heart and life change is always a process."[2]

Lament

Lament is something we seldom talk about, let alone do. It is a common concept in many conversations regarding racial reconciliation. It is the first step in acknowledging or expressing a wrong or injustice done. Lament is genuinely mourning for offenses committed against another. It is one thing to express sorrow; it is quite another to own it, to feel it, to actually lament. Lamenting is essential to the process of forgiveness, reconciliation, and restoration of peace in a relationship. It is one thing to lament a personal sin or offense against someone and is entirely different to lament sins of injustice and oppression of one race against another.

> *In my heart of hearts I want us to be able to make it through the*
> *wall of lament and see the joy that awaits us at the finish line.*
> *We will rejoice together praising Him for the victory.*
> —John Perkins

I'm taking on the delicate matter of the collective sins of the White race against the Black race and, quite frankly, all races. It is extremely difficult to properly acknowledge the sinful injustices committed over a century ago by my White ancestors if I cannot feel the pain of those who carry the burden of our past. The problem White people have with lamenting is we don't really know how to lament properly and effectively the sin of slavery committed over a hundred years ago. It is impossible for people—in this case, Whites— to empathize, to feel what someone has been through or is going through, without experiencing the same or something similar.

Divorced people understand to a greater degree the pain in the loss of a marriage than someone who is not divorced. A child of divorce experiences pain that a child whose mom and dad stay together cannot grasp. It is easier said than done, and unless we make an effort to empathize—to walk a mile in their shoes, so to speak—we will be limited in our ability to truly lament for the offenses done to the ancestors of our Black friends.

It takes befriending and building relational equity and trust with someone who is Black to gain the knowledge to genuinely empathize and lament. I have discovered from my friends of color that they talk differently when they are among their people than they do when they are among Whites. The only way for your friends of color to relax and be themselves when they are around you is to spend more time together. Time together allows people to overcome any misgivings about offending each other. When allowed inside each other's circle of trust, the eyes of the heart will begin to see their world, the historical challenges of being Black, and the challenges they face on a daily basis as a Black man or woman navigating a system established by mostly White people. It also gives people of color insight into the heart choosing to see beyond the color of their skin. It takes effort and is uncomfortable at first, but it is worth it if your heart's desire is to know and understand deeper those of another color or ethnicity. It is amazing what God reveals when we choose to enter the divide. It is in the divide that God reveals the exceeding riches of His grace.

It's a heart thing, and kindred hearts find a lane of trust and communication that just works. Once they move past the fear of offending each other, new friends will enjoy each other. The greatest gift we can give to each other is to relax and be ourselves. We learn to see things from each other's perspective, and that will help us in the process of lamenting. Knowing each other's heart is key to mutual trust and rich friendships. We are different in so many ways, but as we respect and celebrate each other's differences, we can continue to be our unique selves and even celebrate our differences.

> Knowing each other's heart is key to mutual trust and rich friendships.

On my third visit to Tuskegee University, I was in the office of archivist Dana Chandler. Dana and I were getting to know each other on a deeper level. As we talked about my book idea, I made the statement that, for the book to be credible, it required the love and mercy of God as well as influence from friends of color. I knew any book written by an old White guy had to have eyes on it by people with Black skin. Without hesitation, Dana said, "You need to know Charlie." Charlie

Vincent is a Church of Christ preacher in Monticello, Arkansas, and has two sons who graduated from Tuskegee University.

Dana connected Charlie and me, and on my way back to Fort Worth from Tuskegee, I took a side trip to Monticello to meet Charlie and his wife, Bennie. We sat in the sanctuary of Kennedy Boulevard Church of Christ and just visited. As we talked, they began to tell me a little of their story. They described how their church was born out of the ugliness (my word) of the supposed best of my people. By "ugly," I am referring to how White people in the church treated Charlie and Bennie. By "best," I am referring to men and women, leaders in the church, who professed to be Christians but behaved like Christ was nowhere around. It reminds me of what the prophet Jeremiah said: "You are always on their lips but far from their hearts" (Jeremiah 12:2, NIV).

Charlie and Bennie were baptized in 1978 by a Church of Christ preacher, who happened to be White. He baptized them at the church in Monticello, which was also White and was the only Church of Christ in town. A few weeks later, the preacher who baptized them was fired. It seems the elders just couldn't handle a Black couple being baptized in their lily-White church. They must have missed Matthew 28:19, where Jesus said, "Go therefore and make disciples of all the nations, baptizing them in the name of the Father and of the Son and of the Holy Spirit." Stories like this make me so ashamed of my people. This was not in the fifties or sixties. This incident happened in the late seventies. I cannot bear to think that such prejudice is still in our midst today, but I know it is.

> I cannot bear to think that such prejudice is still in our midst today, but I know it is.

You may have noticed I refer to the White race as "my people." I borrowed that phrase from Dr. Washington. He always considered himself a representative of his race. His reference to the people of his race in that way has influenced me to think about how I represent my race, my country, my people. Does the way I treat people of color confirm or deny who I am in Christ?

As Charlie and I became friends, our trust in each other grew, and we moved beyond any fear of offending each other. Our conversations regarding the history of both races became routine and were always genuine and respectful. One day we were engaged in conversation when Charlie asked me if I had seen the movie *Something the Lord Made*. I said no, and he suggested that Dianne and I watch it. It is an amazing true story, and I will not go into it other than to say it is a must-see. Charlie has recommended many movies to me, and watching them helps me have a deeper understanding of what it means to navigate life in a world that opposes you because of the color of your skin. When we watch a movie, we experience what a character in the movie experiences. When he loves, we love. When he or she experiences mistreatment, we feel the pain. Other movies that will help you learn to lament deeply and authentically are *A Lesson Before Dying*, *The Best of Enemies*, *The Last Brickmaker in America*, and *Same Kind of Different as Me*. Movies are very effective tools for learning to lament with empathy.

One of my buddies who happens to be Black is Marcus White. Marcus knows Dianne is an early-to-bedder, so one evening he invited me over to watch a movie. The movie was *12 Years a Slave*. About an hour into the movie, the scenes of horrific treatment from White people to their Black slaves were just about all I could stand. When I had seen enough, I turned to Marcus and said, "I hate White people." Marcus laughed, but it created in me a feeling of lament like I had never experienced before. It was in that moment that I understood the reality of bitterness toward White people in general that carries such a heavy burden for members of the Black race.

This is a big deal in our quest for reconciliation. For a Black person, it requires an extra measure of grace not to judge, distrust, and misinterpret someone who is White. And for White people, an extra measure of grace is required not to be offended when a Black person gives a look of disdain or even hate. We have to own it, turn the other cheek, and not be offended. The best thing we can do is pray and be who Washington would be in that moment—smile and show some heart. Express the love of Jesus to that person who God created in His image. Proverbs 15:1 says, "A soft word turns away wrath."

It takes time together to build relational equity and trust.

To lament requires a deeper knowledge. To learn the deeper truth from someone who doesn't look like us requires a genuine interest in them personally. In conversations with someone who looks different, it is highly unlikely that they will share their darkest moments of being treated badly by someone with White skin. It takes time together to build relational equity and trust. When trust is established and the relationship moves beyond an acquaintance, God will provide moments of truth-sharing. But it is essential that it be on their terms, not forced. And remember, life is not about you, no matter the color of your skin. Be like Booker T. Washington, always serving others.

One truth I have learned in my journey inside the world of my Black friends is every single person with Black skin has a story of mistreatment, oppression, or injustice at the hands of someone under White skin. It's critical to keep that in mind when you are engaging with people of color, and it helps to empathize with a little more kindness. For a White person trying to understand why a person of color gives a bitter eye or a disrespectful gesture, knowing this truth will help him turn the other cheek. The journey down to a level of lamenting humility is uncomfortable and may even be embarrassing when stories are shared of unbelievable treatment of another human being at the hands of someone who looks like you. It can be liberating as well and tills the soil for a friendship of gracious proportions. The friends made along the way who happen to be Black will bring a rich blessing to life and an enlightened spirit that would otherwise never been experienced.

When you lament your loss and pain, your fear and sin, and your loneliness and anger, you will discover that Jesus joins you in that dark place. We are created in His image and we laugh the way He laughs and for the same reasons. His laughter defines ours. Just so, His sadness and tears define ours, too. If we're going to understand our laughter and lament, it starts with God. Everything starts with Him.
—Steve Brown

Repent

Repent is the next step after lament. The word *repent* is very close to the word *lament*. While we are deeply sorry for our behavior or even the behavior of our ancestors, to repent means to change, to reroute one's life, and to move from living in darkness to living in the light. The challenge is to determine what repent means for the change in each of us personally. How our attitude changes toward people who don't look like us depends on how surrendered we are to the will of God. Repentance is unique to each one of us, and with the help of the Holy Spirit, we will be made aware of what changes need to take place in the way we live, in how we treat and receive others, and in emancipating our hearts.

> When we lock hearts and walk the path of life together, something powerful takes place.

In my case, I have had many acquaintances with men of color over the years, but I had no close friendships. I had never given it much thought until I served at Royal Family Kids Camp. I talked earlier about Marcus, my buddy who invited me over for a movie. He was my buddy counselor and has become a great friend. He is crazier than me, and we have had so much fun telling each other stories that have fostered trust. It is through Marcus that my attitude began to change; I realized there are things about me as a White guy that are unique to me, and there are things about Marcus that are unique to him because he is a Black guy. The glory comes when we learn to celebrate our differences to the extent that we have become almost incapable of offending one another. When we lock hearts and walk the path of life together, something powerful takes place. I call it "expanding the borders of grace." If someone thinks they know grace now and have no friends of color, this is swimming in the shallows. To experience the deeper waters of grace, pray for God to bless you with at least one multiethnic friendship.

Marcus and I didn't set out to become friends because one of us was White and the other was Black. We became friends because of who we are in Christ. We both love the Lord; we love kids; and we're goofy as heck. We had so much fun with the boys at camp and laughed a lot, along with some crying too, as we served these kids "together" as brothers, sibling arrows in the quiver of God. As Marcus and I grew closer, we began sharing stuff from each other's perspective that opened our eyes and deepened our friendship. When God's children enter the divide and become a relational blend of His creative design, He is glorified.

Repentance is the process of exposing darkness to light, lies to truth. Honesty before God brings us his undivided attention and his forgiving love. We can't climb our way out of the pit. But when we admit we are in the pit and call for help, the God of grace and truth will deliver us from its deception and destruction.
—Dudley Hall

Implement

Now that I have lamented the sins of my people against God and His children with Black skin, and I have repented of those sins—that is, changed my heart, which has been influenced by generations of my White heritage—what does the transformation of my heart look like? To implement means to fulfill, to perform, or to carry out. So, the question is, "How do I carry out who God has designed me to be when entering the divide and integrating my heart with people of all nations?" It's a simple question with a complex answer because of our uniqueness. It's really not as difficult as we may think, yet because we choose to remain in our comfort zone, we continue to navigate life in the status quo. Most of the time, we simply don't think about it, but we actually should if our heart's desire is to live life "to the full" (John 10:10, NIV), according to the words of Jesus. Our behavior toward each other is born out of what we believe about each other, but it first and foremost is born out of what we believe about God and the finished work of Jesus. Unless we place the King of Kings on the throne of our lives and follow His will, our hearts will never be emancipated.

> By the end of the evening, Alex invited us to come to his mom and dad's the following Sunday for dinner.

Dianne and I had just moved to Kansas City and were having dinner at P.F. Chang's on the Plaza. Our waiter was a Hispanic young man named Alex, in his early twenties. He had a winsome personality and described the entrees and specials like a chef. I got to thinking he probably knew where the best Mexican restaurant was in KC. When I asked Alex where he liked to eat Mexican food, he never hesitated and answered, "My mom's." We laughed and carried on, and throughout the evening, we continued to talk about Mexican food as he served us graciously. By the end of the evening, Alex invited us to come to his mom and dad's the following Sunday for dinner. We accepted, and on Sunday we headed to the barrio to join a family who didn't speak English for dinner. As we walked up the sidewalk to the house, Dianne gave me a look that would make a bulldog break his chain. She was communicating clearly with me, "Don't ever do something like this again." Obviously, she was uncomfortable because we were not exactly in the safest part of our comfort zone, or the safest part of town.

The dinner and fellowship could not have been more enjoyable. Alex and his family served us pork carnitas on homemade tortillas, and we wanted to bring an American dessert, so we made banana pudding. Alex and his girlfriend were the only ones who spoke English. As we departed, Alex's papa said to me, "Mi casa, su casa." Those words literally brought tears to my eyes. Gathering around the table in fellowship with people of a different culture can be a rich experience. Food is good to gather around. Yes, there is risk, but the risk is worth taking for the blessings of conquering the divide. God is love, and Love has only one language, the language of one blood and one race in the kingdom.

When we moved to Fort Worth, one day I was working in the yard when the sanitation truck came down the street. As the men on the back of the truck hopped off to gather the bags by the curb, I walked over to the driver and asked if he would like a bottle of water. He said yes, so I ran in and grabbed two bottles and brought them out. The driver's name is Dexter, and seemingly such a small thing has turned into a routine connection between Dexter and me. Now, his helper Chris engages in a shout-out of one kind or another. When I hear the truck coming down the street, I walk out and hand each of the guys a bottle of water. It is such a small gesture but they appreciate it, and we have become friends.

Why would they do that?

One day, as I was on a walk about a mile from our home, there was an elderly woman in her lawn cleaning up limbs and leaves after a thunderstorm. I stopped to help her with a task that was going to take maybe an hour. Dexter and his crew were coming down the street, and when they saw me, they stopped, jumped off the truck, and proceeded to pick up the leaves and limbs. They loaded them onto the truck in short order and continued on their way. The sweet lady was beside herself and kept asking, "Why would they do that?" You just never know how God will manifest His presence, but He certainly did in that moment. Two bottles of water, twice a week—who'd a thunk it?

These are just a couple of examples of implementing the love of Jesus when entering the divide, making sure someone knows they matter, that they are worthy of dignity, and that they are seen as equal and as brothers. The main thing is to open our hearts to the kindness of our heavenly Father and open our minds to the truth that with every single person we encounter—whether on the street, at work, at church, or at Walmart—we were all created equal in the eyes of God. There is dignity in expressing that truth in how we treat those we encounter. We can be different on the outside yet the same beautiful color under our skin. Be intentional about it in prayer, praying for grace to have a growing heart toward those who don't look like you. Enter the divide and invite someone to breakfast, lunch, or coffee to open the dialogue or simply be kind.

> Love does not look for causes; it looks for persons.

It may feel awkward at first because any time we step out of our comfort zone, it is always uncomfortable. But it is an acquired taste that gets sweeter as our friendships grow. When our heart integrates with the heart of another, God will reveal His love in those friendships. There is only one thing worth giving our lives for, and that is relationships motivated by love. Love does not look for causes; it looks for persons.

Fear

Fear plays a big part in holding us back. There is not a single one of us who hasn't stopped short of doing the right thing when an opportunity to step up presented itself. We stop short because we are afraid we will offend someone, or we fear what people think. This is especially true when it comes to entering the no-go zone regarding race. I am guilty as charged, and if my friend A. J., who happens to be Black, had not set me straight, I might still be holding back when the truth needs to be spoken. A. J. is retired from the Detroit police department, and we became friends working on the set of *The Chosen*. We were talking about racial stuff one day, and I made a statement but followed it up with, "I can't really say that publicly because I'm White." A. J. was quick to say, "That is BS," and proceeded to let me know that what I said was the truth, and if a Black person gets offended by it because it came from a White man, he is making it more about skin than sin. He also asked why I thought I could say it to him and not another Black person. I explained that we know each other well enough that we can be candid regarding what is true and what is not.

When I thought about it, I realized it is fear that keeps us from speaking up when God has provided an opportunity to say or do the right thing. The enemy has convinced us, especially White folks, that anything we say can be used against us in the court of public opinion, and the verdict is "you're a racist." The greatest fear of someone with White skin is to be called a racist—unless you simply don't care.

I am reminded of the relationship between President Theodore Roosevelt and Booker T. Washington. Roosevelt and Booker had become friends, and out of that relationship, Teddy had begun to rely on Booker for advice regarding the Black race and how the two races could work together. Booker was in a position to counsel the president regarding appointments of the best and brightest Black candidates as well as high-character Whites for positions in Roosevelt's administration. The president was further along in his acceptance of Blacks and had no anxiety regarding their abilities and usefulness. Teddy was much more racially progressive than the masses in America, especially in the South. Having grown up with a dad who had a heart for the downtrodden and fighting alongside Black men and Native Americans on San Juan Hill in Cuba contributed to Teddy's ideology of equality.

This difference between Teddy and the American people was never clearer than when the news of his hosting a Black man for dinner at the White House hit the streets. I will not go into the details of the dinner, which was attended by the entire Roosevelt family, but there is a great book, *Teddy and Booker T* by Brian Kilmeade, that explores in much greater detail the relationship between the two icons, who were ahead of their time in a divided nation.

The backlash from the news of the dinner was one Teddy never expected. Booker was not surprised, given his history growing up as a slave and navigating the waters of White supremacy in a world opposed to the man farthest down. After that dinner, fear created anxiety in the president regarding his popularity among his mostly White voter base. That same fear led Teddy to make an error in judgment regarding an incident in Brownsville, Texas, when a group of Buffalo Soldiers had been accused of killing a White man, and the case was inadequately investigated. Because of the White House dinner backlash, Teddy continued to give in to fear rather than doing the right thing. He had the Black soldiers dismissed with no pension. The details of this story are in Kilmeade's book as well.

The following is borrowed from *Teddy and Booker T.* and gives us a good description of the outcome of fear and how it can manipulate the judgment of an otherwise courageous man of integrity.

> For better or for worse, the White House dinner and the Brownsville episode were defining moments in the narrative of Booker's and Theodore's brave—but ultimately imperfect—relationship. Once and for all, the Texas controversy signaled an end to their

valiant joint effort to effect change in the country
for the Black man.[3]

We can only guess where we would be today had President
Roosevelt stood his ground and embraced what was in his heart
regarding Booker T. Washington and his race. I believe President
Roosevelt truly wanted to move forward racially and had no idea
his inviting Booker T. Washington for dinner would play out with
such an ugly outcome. The president knew in his heart the right
thing to do, yet he succumbed to pressure from the outside that
altered his true identity on the inside.

Trust

Fear is a lack of trust, and the only way to build trust is spending
time together. In my friendship with A.J., the reason we can say
things to each other that may offend someone else is trust and
relational equity. It takes time together to build both. We must go
deeper in our relationships. Skin-deep friendships won't cut it.

Spending time together is key to building and rebuilding trust.
We can connect with friends through email, texting, and social
media, but it's not the same as being together in person. Hearts
must be in close proximity for the dynamic of trust to grow, and
intimacy happens when rich conversations and prayer are shared.
The outcome of what is revealed when we are together determines
whether trust grows. Trust will never be restored apart from time
together.

For someone who is Black, the thought of spending time with
someone who is White may sound risky and would certainly be a
step out of one's comfort zone. Until a person decides to take the
risk, God's rewards will remain unrealized. As you place your trust
in God, He will reveal the joy available by trusting someone who is
White. He may also reveal that this trust is not for all White people.
What determines trustworthiness in a person is on the inside, in the

heart. My good friend Charlie Vincent said his parents raised him to believe that all Whites are not your enemy, and all Blacks are not your friend. It is not the color of our skin that determines whether we can be trusted. It is what is on the inside, a person's character and heart, that determines trustworthiness.

We lack trust, pure and simple.

Consider what is printed on our currency: "In God We Trust." In reality, this is rarely if ever considered. We have abandoned God, like Adam and Eve in the Garden of Eden, and it has led us to where we are today, a culture rife with fatherlessness, crime, immorality, and confusion regarding the reality of God's design and His best for us. We lack trust, pure and simple. We no longer trust God, and without trusting Him, we do not trust each other.

Think about how we have abandoned God and His moral order in so many ways, especially in the institutions of our land. We removed the Ten Commandments from courtrooms and public buildings across the land. We removed prayer from the classroom and made it illegal to force or require students to recite the Pledge of Allegiance to the flag. We have allowed our classrooms to be transformed from a place of educating our kids to indoctrinating them with an ideology that is anti-God and has no place in a civilized culture. These are just a few of the ways we have told God we no longer want Him or need Him to be a part of our culture and who we are, even though America was founded on belief in God and biblical principles. The decision to remove God from the public square set America on the path of self-destruction, no longer trusting in God and each other.

Persons who have a common purpose
may still maintain helpful, friendly relations,
even if they do differ as to details and
choose to travel to the common goal by different roads.
—Booker T. Washington

How do we expect to trust each other when we have chosen to break trust with the One who created us? As He demonstrated with Adam and Eve in the Garden, God gives us the freedom to choose. We can live a life that is either destructive or according to His will. Unfortunately, too often we make the wrong choice. We see evidence of choosing to follow God in the building of Tuskegee Institute.

The "corner-stone" in the following quote refers to the cornerstone in the foundation of Porter Hall, the first building erected on the campus of Tuskegee Institute in 1883. This was a miracle of God's grace and love for the man farthest down. It was built by the students and was the first of many buildings to be erected on the campus of the growing institute. This process of development began with a thought, an idea of former slave Lewis Adams and former slave owner George Campbell. These two men, one Black and one White, answered God's call, together, that continues to bless mankind today.

> When it is considered that the laying of this corner-stone took place in the heart of the South, in the "Black Belt," in the centre of that part of our country that was most devoted to slavery; that at that time slavery had been abolished only about sixteen years; that only sixteen years before that no Negro could be taught from books without the teacher receiving the condemnation of the law or of public sentiment—when all this is considered, the scene that was witnessed on that spring day at Tuskegee was a remarkable one. I believe there are few places in the world where it could have taken place.[4]

Few things can help an individual more than to place responsibility on him, and to let him know that you trust him.
—Booker T. Washington

CHAPTER TWELVE

Emancipation Grace

*We cannot "psychologize" the grace of
God. God's actions are outside and above
our human sciences.*
—John Joseph Powell

Free from Me

Setting yourself free from the bondage of yourself is a daunting task, but it is the ultimate gift of grace. It is also a tremendous blessing to your friends and especially your family. It took the story of Booker T. Washington to help me come to grips with my blind spots, afflictions, and all the other ways the enemy of God controlled the affections of my heart. Because of Christ, who shined in the life of Booker, I came face-to-face with my demons and gradually began to see clearly the man God created me to be. The real education began when I hit bottom, as God revealed how I was allowing the enemy to destroy our family through me. It was there that the words of Booker T. Washington—"it is at the bottom of life we must begin"[1]—began to make sense. I learned that the view from the bottom gives you a most vivid picture of the reality of what is most important in life: your relationships, both vertical and horizontal.

For most of my seventy-two years on planet Earth, I have lived in the city. I love the outdoors and am extremely comfortable in the wilderness, whether going solo or with a friend alongside. Whether standing in a trout stream in Montana with my fly rod in hand, chasing elk with my bow and arrow, shooting bears with my camera in the Alaska bush, or sitting in the turkey woods on a crisp spring morning, I am in my happy place. Or so I thought. Looking in the rearview mirror, I now see all of those wonderful experiences had become idols. I became aware that over most of my life, it had been me going somewhere to do something. My identity was more about the things I did than who I was becoming.

I would have loved to have known earlier in my life what I know now, but life doesn't work that way. Only by grace did I come to know the details of Dr. Washington's life when I acquired a copy of *Up from Slavery*. It should be required reading in history classes, and especially in our homes. His story is inspirational and will call your children to greater appreciate the value of education and that reading is the anecdote for ignorance. They will learn the importance of building character, that hard work pays off and can actually be fun, and that the greatest joy comes when we help others.

> **The truth is, Dr. Washington was too smart for the people of all races.**

Since learning about Washington, I often wonder where we would be today had we adopted his teachings and methods. All Americans—Blacks, Whites, and even Native Americans—are guilty of ignoring the path of wisdom and character that Washington blazed. The truth is, Dr. Washington was too smart for the people of all races. Though his skin was Black, he was head and shoulders above all others of his time. His methods were grounded in education and the principles of independence and self-reliance. Our ancestors of both races could not see the wisdom in his ways, or else they simply chose not to believe it.

What is hard for us to accept about Booker T. Washington's success is that it begins with forgiveness and his methods take time. The process that lasts—the long way—is slow, steadfast, and principled. In today's world, people prefer the convenience of immediate gratification, and our country is paying the price. Ignorance is at an all-time high because we have allowed it to happen, not just in our institutions of higher learning but in our homes as well. We must return to the idea that when we raise a child, we are growing an adult. That boy or girl is in the process of maturing. Booker T. Washington began a process with the end in mind. We must do the same, whether raising kids, managing ourselves, or building a school, business, or church. We must know where we are going.

> *Yes, your life is messy and hard, but that's not a failure of the plan; it is the plan. It's God working to complete what he's begun in you.*
> —Paul David Tripp, New Morning Mercies

Forgiveness

> So watch yourselves. "If your brother or sister sins against you, rebuke them; and if they repent, forgive them. Even if they sin against you seven times in a day and seven times come back to you saying, 'I repent,' you must forgive them." (Luke 17:3-4, NIV)

These words from Jesus are a good example of how we pay little or no attention to Scripture, even the words of Jesus. These words not only offend us, but they sound ridiculous in terms of our own justice system. It pains me to forgive, but that is what we are commanded to do by our Lord. Forgiveness is an acquired taste, and it takes time for the idea of forgiving someone who has sinned against you to become palatable to the mind.

This one thing—forgiveness—is what set Booker T. Washington apart and was at the core of what made him so successful. I cannot imagine what he had to overcome in his heart to have such a compassionate view of the ones who had oppressed, enslaved, and committed horrific acts of violence against his people. But that is exactly what he did. He forgave and never allowed himself to hate. The following quote is the spirit of forgiveness that dwelled in the heart of Booker T. Washington:

> Of all forms of slavery there is none that is so harmful and degrading as that form of slavery which tempts one human being to hate another by reason of his race or color.[2]

Washington recognized early on that to forgive was to release himself from the ultimate bondage of bitterness. Bitterness is at the core of why we have so much hate between the races. Jesus' words to forgive seven times in a day were spoken in general terms with specific outcomes. You are to take those words to heart and forgive the person who comes to mind as you read this. It may be a family thing, a work thing, or a marital thing. Then again, it may be a race thing, where you hold an entire race hostage to your own chains of bitterness. Because Booker T. Washington chose to live in a constant state of forgiveness, he was blessed with opportunities that were a harvest of glory.

If you are Black, you have every right to be untrusting of anyone with White skin. White people have a history of committing sins of oppression and injustice to those wearing every color of skin on planet Earth. My hope is that you will look beyond the color of my skin and receive the message here as if it came from one of your own. After all, I am one of your own as a sibling in God's family. It is important that we believe what Booker T. Washington said in the above quote. If you are in bondage to bitterness, you are a slave, and the only way you will ever allow good thoughts about someone with White skin is to forgive. Booker knew this, and he lived each day with a forgiving spirit—and it blessed him and the world immeasurably. According to David Takle, author of *The Truth About Lies and Lies About Truth*, our emotions and responses come out of how we interpret a situation. David said, "In truth the person's anger comes from his or her own interpretation of what was going on."[3]

No one goes through life without being wounded. Jesus told us how to deal with those wounds, and Booker not only believed his Savior, but he forgave as he had been forgiven. It is important that we don't confuse forgiveness with reconciliation. They are two different things. Forgiveness is a one-way street. I can forgive someone who has no interest in reconciliation. The person you forgive may not even be alive anymore. While it only takes one to forgive, reconciliation takes at least two people with a heartfelt desire for restoration for it to come to pass.

You and I must forgive. We have no choice in the matter. Jesus Christ made the choice for us when He bore your sins and mine on the cross. When you take up your cross, you give up your right as creditor. You've been wounded by someone who has failed to give you what you believe is due. You're due an explanation. You're due an apology. You're due some respect or a promise kept or some faithfulness. You have not received what you are due. To follow Jesus, you don't have to forget, but you must forgive. You may even believe you are due reparations, but Jesus repaired it all, including the sins against you at the hands of someone with White skin.

Forgiveness is the most difficult of all the things Jesus said we must do in order to enter the kingdom. While we'd prefer to be a people who demand what we are due, we must embrace the unfairness of the Gospel. If God was all about keeping the books, then all we would need is Moses and the law. But God is all about grace, and that's why we need Jesus and the cross. In Ephesians 1:4-7, the apostle Paul pointed out that Jesus chose to bear what we deserve by sacrificing His right for our wrongs. We must never lose the wonder of the Gospel and what is critical to getting along as God would have it. It matters that we get along, so much so that God interpreted Himself to the world by walking among us to love, forgive, and serve all nations.

We must return grace because we have received grace. Jesus told a story in Matthew 18 about a king who graciously erased the debt of a servant, but the servant, in turn, demanded a fellow servant pay him the debt owed. None of us can pay our debt to God, but the King forgives—and so must we. When we take communion, we are reminded that the King forgave us, even with all of our sin-filled baggage. How can we receive the unlimited grace of God yet refuse to extend it to our offenders and claim to have any resemblance to our Lord? This does not diminish the badness of a sin against us but proclaims the goodness of God, who forgives all of our sins. Jesus doesn't expect you to forget the wound; He just wants you to remember it the right way.

> Therefore, as the elect of God, holy and beloved, put on tender mercies, kindness, humility, meekness, longsuffering; bearing with one another, and forgiving one another, if anyone has a complaint against another; even as Christ forgave you, so you also must do. (Colossians 3:12-13)

When we give up our right for retaliation, we are pursuing the best possible way to make things right. After all, is it not peace that we all desire?

We must believe in the power of good. Forgiving is not endorsing passivity; it is intentionally choosing to respond to evil with aggressive goodness. When has retaliation ever worked in producing reconciliation? In Luke 6:27, Jesus said, "Love your enemies; do good to those who hate you." Retaliation does not lead to reconciliation; forgiveness does.

Here's the deal. If the Gospel is wrong, it is up to you to get revenge, fight back, be bitter, or whatever way you choose to retaliate. If the Gospel is wrong, it is up to you to make it right and get revenge. But if the Gospel is true, it's up to God. No one will get away with anything. All sin is going to be judged. Only God is qualified to do the judging. When you decide to do the judging, you are in contempt of court. Making things right is God's job. It says in 1 Peter 2:23 that Jesus never retaliated. When you release your wounder to God, you are actually releasing yourself.

Generational bitterness may be at the core of your stronghold of unforgiveness, and if it is, you are in bondage to it. You are a slave to the sin of unforgiveness. Jesus wants us to live an emancipated life of true freedom. When Jesus says you must forgive, He is actually liberating you. Bitterness is to the soul what cancer is to the body. It closes your heart to healing and opens wide the door for the enemy of God to pursue you relentlessly.

This is what the apostle Paul was talking about when he said, "Do not give the devil a foothold" (Ephesians 4:27, NIV). The enemy is looking for a way to get into your very soul and drain your life of joy and all things good. But Paul encouraged the church at Ephesus with these words:

> Get rid of all bitterness, rage and anger, brawling and slander, along with every form of malice. Be kind and compassionate to one another, forgiving each other, just as in Christ God forgave you. (Ephesians 4:31-32, NIV)

Don't let your wound become your identity. You can't change the past, and you don't have to be chained to it either. I am reminded of what Lionel Richie said regarding the past: "When your past calls, don't answer. It has nothing new to say."[4] King Jesus came to set us free, and He knows freedom requires forgiveness.

I love good stories, especially the ones with a heartfelt message. Stories bring the reality of life into our minds and influence the condition of our hearts. If you are not White, it is easy to justify unforgiveness for people with White skin. That is a simple fact because sin has manifested itself in people with White skin in ways we cannot count. Only you can identify those with White skin whom you believe have sinned against you.

An exercise that may help you forgive people for simply being born White is to visualize Bob Goff. 1 can think of no other White man who walks on planet Earth today that 1 would nominate to represent my race than Bob. If you don't know about Bob Goff, do yourself a favor and check out his book *Love Does*. Watch some of his YouTube videos, and you will find he exuberantly reflects the love of God. Bob is goofy, and that may be what 1 love the most. He lives in kingdom mode 24/7. One story that will capture your attention is Bob's pursuit of bringing witch doctors to justice in Uganda. The outcome of his love for the Ugandan people is that the government of Uganda named Bob Goff an Honorary Consul to the Republic of Uganda. When you have the urge to give the bitter eye to someone White, think of Jesus first, then think of Bob Goff. That little pause will help your heart settle down and not allow skin color to influence how you treat someone, let alone forgive them.

Forgiveness is a choice. If Jesus is Lord, forgiveness is your only choice. Choose not to focus on what someone has done to you, but choose instead to focus on what Jesus has done for you. How you and 1 respond to our wounder must be shaped by how Jesus responded to His wounders, which includes you and me. 1 choose to find my identity in the One who was wounded for me. Forgiveness is the hardest of all, yet it is the environment of God. If Jesus is Lord of all, He is Lord of all your wounds.

Forgiveness may not bring your wounder into the kingdom, but it will move you closer to the throne. 1 choose to live each day with a spirit of forgiveness.

> *Memory makes it possible for us both to bless the past,*
> *even those parts of it that we have always felt*
> *cursed by, and also to be blessed by it . . .*
> *what the forgiveness of sins is all about.*
> —Brennan Manning

Mercy

"Jesus, Son of David, have mercy on me!" These were the words of Bartimaeus as he sat, begging, on the roadside outside of Jericho. Jesus was passing by with His disciples and a large crowd. When Jesus heard the man cry out, He stopped and called for the man. As the story goes, Bartimaeus was led to Jesus, and Jesus asked, "What do you want Me to do for you?" The blind man said to Him, "Rabboni, that I might receive my sight." Jesus said to him, "Go your way; your faith has made you well." And immediately Bartimaeus received his sight and followed Jesus on the road.

You may want to read the full story in Mark 10:46-52. As the words sink in, think about how we are so much like Bartimaeus in our most basic need for mercy. Mercy is the outcome of the loving-kindness of God to a sinful and depraved world.

> *Mercy is what we have been given*
> *and what we are called to give.*
> —Paul David Tripp

We rarely give thought to Scriptures like this because it requires a gesture toward others that makes us uncomfortable. It requires an action we find difficult and too often impossible, even though God has so graciously given to us. Why are we so reluctant to have mercy on others when we have been so blessed by the mercy of God? How is it that we fail to respond in love to others when we are renewed every day by the love of God?

James 1:20 says, "For the wrath of man does not produce the righteousness of God." If the wrath of man does not produce the righteousness of God, then what does it produce? It produces anger. So, what produces the righteousness of God? Surrendering our will for the will of the Father and declaring Jesus Christ as our Lord and Savior. He paid for every sin, every offense, and every injustice against every single one of us. I know it is hard to believe, but He even paid for the sins of White people. He even paid the debt for whatever it is you hold against someone in your life. That includes every relational sin from and against you, even racial injustice and the bitter hold it has on your heart. To have mercy is to be like Christ.

Being gentle with the heart of a restored sinner is not always done according to Scripture in our churches. This is the biblical command found in Galatians 6:1: "Brothers and sisters, if someone is caught in a sin, you who live by the Spirit should restore that person gently" (NIV). No one wants to be around people who think they are better, and quite frankly, sinners are often uncomfortable in church because they are made to feel like they do not belong. Hmm. Are we not all sinners? Are we not all in need of mercy? Until we own our own need for mercy, we will find it hard to be merciful.

> *Oh, give thanks to the LORD, for He is good!*
> *For His mercy endures forever.*
> —Psalm 136:1

The same is true when it comes to the racial divide. Centuries of being treated as "less than" have created bitterness toward Whites from every race. Typically, Whites don't understand this because they have difficulty empathizing with something they have never experienced. This is hard for White folks to hear, and I don't even like saying it. It is historically true that we have lived with privileges we take for granted because they have always been available to us with White skin. I was probably accepted to Harding College, now University, in 1970 because I was White. When I graduated high school, I didn't have the grades nor any redeeming values that would qualify me for acceptance at a school with high academic requirements. But because I was White and my parents knew a guy, I was accepted. Given the same set of circumstances with a Black student whose grades and character were excellent, he may have been denied. I have no doubt about this.

One of the greatest blessings from my Tuskegee journey has

been discovering how oblivious we've been about engaging with those who don't look like us. We tend to operate in our White world without any thought of making friends with people of color. And my black friends don't get a pass because they do it too. They like being with their own, just like the rest of us. This is something that each one of us must answer for ourselves. You may disagree, but let's dig a little deeper to find out.

1. How many close friends, not acquaintances, do you have that are a different race than you?
2. How often do you have coffee, lunch, or dinner or golf, hunt, fish, etc. with a friend who does not look like you?

If you can answer either of these questions with any number other than a zero, you are the exception. As a rule, White folks don't have close friends with people of color, which includes Native Americans, as well as Hispanic, Asian, and Jewish people, or any of God's other children. To get down to bedrock, as Booker T. Washington called it, all of us, regardless of the color of our skin, do this to some degree because it comes naturally. Not including people who don't look like us in our regular orbit is certainly not sinful, but I do believe we miss the deeper and richer relational opportunities that God graciously provides when we allow our circle of friends to include people of color. When we do so, I believe we gain broader insights of wisdom and knowledge that God provides when we choose to seek His grace by erasing the racial boundaries that divide us.

Why do we tend to stick with those who look like us? Like I said before, it's in our nature. Most Blacks have few, if any, White friends, and most Whites have few, if any, Black friends. We have acquaintances of color but not "hanging out" friends whom we engage with on a regular basis. My opinion is that we don't create opportunities to get to know others who don't look like us. It's not a Black thing, and it's not a White thing. It's just something we don't think about. It is an unconscious thing we do, both Blacks and Whites. But I promise you this: you will be blessed when you step into the unknown and invite someone who doesn't look like you for coffee or lunch. I can't really explain what happens; I just know that God shows up, and it is good, with few exceptions. Whites in general make little or no effort to make friends with people of color because the idea never enters their mind. The term "unconscious bias" may apply here, but I think a more accurate description is "unconscious segregation" or "negligent segregation," which is a boundary the enemy has placed in our minds that we are unaware of.

I have White friends who I guarantee will deny such an admonition, yet they would never entertain the idea of becoming close friends with a person of color. The very idea here will be uncomfortable for most Whites and Blacks alike to consider, but I believe it is essential to racial and relational peace in America. When we comprehend how important it is that the righteousness of God is produced in us, and when we discover how good it is, we will seek more of it.

Our need for mercy was born on the day sin entered the world in the Garden of Eden. Everything that divides us relationally also entered creation on that day, including our racial divide. It is in the divide that divine grace brings us together as one. Mercy requires nothing from the sinner, for which I am eternally grateful. Whether your problem is with a family member, a friend, or an entire race of God's children, you must decide whether you will be a conduit of God's mercy or a manifestation of the wrath of man, which "does not produce the righteousness of God" (James 1:20).

In Matthew 5:7, Jesus said, "Blessed are the merciful, for they shall obtain mercy," and in Luke 6:36, Jesus said, "Be merciful, just as your Father also is merciful." It is a tough choice, but it is a choice each one of us must make. Either we choose to have mercy or we hold on to what comes naturally and leave our souls at risk. It is only by the grace of our Lord and Savior, Jesus Christ, that we will choose to become a mercy giver like our Lord. I encourage you to pray to become merciful, like God. As you pray to become like Him, you will be shown mercy and you will glorify God. In the following quote from Psalm 86, King David described our merciful God and how being merciful in heart is to be like Christ.

> But You, O Lord, are a God full of compassion, and gracious,
> longsuffering and abundant in mercy and truth.
> (Psalm 86:15)

What is critical to know about the grace of mercy is that when you allow yourself to have mercy on someone, you are actually having mercy on yourself. Mercy always triumphs over judgment, according to the apostle James:

> For judgment is without mercy to the one who has shown no mercy.
> Mercy triumphs over judgment.
> (James 2:13)

Be Anxious for Nothing

If you have made it this far, you've read the redemptive story of Booker T. Washington and Tuskegee, a story from our history that is accurate and provides many life lessons. You have knowledge that you didn't have before you picked up this book. My question is "What will you do with what you have learned?" Will what you now know make any difference in your life and how you engage with people who may not look like you? Will you choose to make a difference in the world?

Throughout this book, I have shared how my heart was transformed by the teachings of Booker T. Washington. The reason I was drawn to the truth of his teachings is a testament to where his wisdom, character, and humility came from. What came out of Booker originated on the day Jesus rose from the dead. Because Booker surrendered his life to Jesus and the power of the resurrection, he was rarely if ever anxious in his dealings with people of any race. When Jesus said to "turn to them the other cheek also" (Matthew 5:39, NIV), Washington believed it and lived it.

To me, turning the other cheek has always meant that when someone hits you, don't hit them back. Turn the other cheek, and smile when they give the other side a whack. As I read *Up from Slavery*, *Character Building*, and *My Larger Education*, I became increasingly more aware that the main thing that set Booker T. Washington apart was the will to turn the other cheek. To my knowledge he was never attacked, and while Jesus' words may have included a physical encounter of some kind, His exhortation to turn the other cheek referred more to the internal battle that is constantly taking place in our encounters with others.

There is no limit to the examples of turning the other cheek. Thanksgiving was a few weeks ago, and I did something I'd never considered doing in previous years. I talked less and listened more. I actually did a lot of the cooking, which kept me in the kitchen, out of the conversations going on in the den. Dianne and I agreed that this was the most peaceful family gathering we have had in years. I have no doubt that learning to sit down inside, as I believe Washington did in most every instance, had a huge impact on my newfound peace. Learning to recognize the anxiety to express my opinion, when it really doesn't matter, was a huge influencer in the outcome. The goal of every encounter with someone, whether at work, school, church, home, or on the street, should be to close the encounter peacefully.

The Origin of Racism

Have you ever wondered why we don't call anti-Semitism "racism"? Would you not agree that the core of anti-Semitism is indeed racism against the Jews? When we talk about racism, we only talk in terms of the oppression of Blacks by those of the White race. Racism is not an outcome of slavery, nor did it originate in America. So, if racism did not originate in America, where did it come from?

You can follow the sin of race and prejudice all the way back to the Garden of Eden, shortly after Adam and Eve believed the serpent when he lied to them about God. The Bible does not tell us the origin of evil, but when we search the Scriptures, God's Word reveals the origin of racism, which is rooted in evil. The essence of evil is hate. Evil hates creation because it is the work of God. Satan is all about destroying creation and everything in it, which includes you and me. After the fall, God met with Satan, Adam, and Eve. He told them what was going to happen as a result of man's disobedience. God told Adam (man) that he would eat his bread by the sweat of his brow. In other words, labor was going to make man's life difficult. Eve (woman) was going to have pain in childbirth. And He told the serpent he was going to crawl on the ground and eat dust.

God went on to tell them what the future holds. God said He was going to let the seed of woman (human beings) crush the head of Satan. God told Satan he was going to bruise the heel of man.[5] Satan's hatred for God is found all through Scripture. On down the road, Abraham entered the picture, and God told Abraham, "It is through you and your family that the seed will come which will crush the head of Satan" (see Genesis 12).

Satan hates the seed of Abraham because it was that seed (Jesus Christ) that crushed his head. Satan hates Jews because his head was crushed when Jesus, who was a Jew, died on the cross. This is the essence of anti-Semitism and thus the origin of racism. Satan sees the Jews as the instrument God chose that would crush his head. This is not just brother against brother, like Cain and Abel, but race against race, like the Jews and the Gentiles. This is why hate for the Jews is not only the origin of what dwells in the heart of a racist, but hate for God is at the core of our sin nature. We come into the world with it, and unless we surrender our will to the will of the Father through the finished work of Jesus, we will remain in bondage to ourselves and our skinfulness.

That defeat of the enemy on the cross gave God the privilege of forgiving sinners. Because Jesus paid for sin, He could forgive sinners. God is not tolerant; He is merciful. Jesus is the cure for everything that divides us. When you choose to forgive, there is no pushback, no response that makes sense, and no argument because to argue with forgiveness is to argue with grace. To argue with grace is to argue with God, and while we all are guilty in this regard, it is not our best interpretation of the love of God.

The good news of the New Testament is that what Jesus did on the cross gives you and me the capacity to replicate what He did, which is to forgive. When you are offended, you can stop evil by forgiving and having mercy on the one who has offended you. In essence, you hold the keys to your own jail cell, which is mercy. When you forgive, you open the door to the prison of yourself, and by the grace of God, you are free at last. The evil you have stopped is the evil that hates God and His children. Evil seeks revenge for any and all injustices. Evil is defeated at the God level, and it gets defeated at the human level when we choose to forgive. God has armed us with the greatest power in the world, which is the power to forgive. That is how you stop evil.

Forgiveness is the environment of God, and it is critical to climate change in our overheated world of differences. The color of our skin has no bearing on our true identity unless we make it so. I can forgive you for not being exactly like me, and you can forgive me for not being exactly like you. It's a choice—and when we choose to forgive, the temperature in our relationships becomes much more pleasant.

PART IV

Restoration Grace

America's present need is not heroics, but healing;
not nostrums, but normalcy; not revolution, but restoration.
—Warren G. Harding

CHAPTER THIRTEEN

The Renewing of Your Mind

And do not be conformed to this world, but be transformed
by the renewing of your mind, that you may prove what is that
good and acceptable and perfect will of God.
—Romans 12:2

Reviving the Tuskegee Spirit in America

Dr. Washington firmly established a mystique, a vision, a unifying principle for all who entered the hallowed halls of Tuskegee Institute. He recognized and acknowledged the "Tuskegee spirit" at the heart level of the Tuskegee experiment.

In one of his Sunday evening messages to the students and faculty at Tuskegee, as the school year was coming to a close, Dr. Washington said the following:

> I want you to go out in a spirit of liberality toward the white people with whom you come in contact. That is an important matter. When I say this I do not mean that you shall go lowering your manhood or your dignity. Go in a manly way, in a straightforward and honourable way, and then you will show the white people that you are not of a belittling race, that the prejudice which so many people possess cannot come among you and those with whom you work. If you can extend a helping

hand to a white person, feel just as happy in doing so as in helping a black person.

In the sight of God there is no colour line, and we want to cultivate a spirit that will make us forget that there is such a line anywhere. We want to be larger and broader than the people who would oppress us on account of our colour.

No one ever loses anything by being a gentleman or a lady. No person ever lost anything by being broad. Remember that if we are kind and useful, if we are moral, if we go out and practise these traits, no matter what people say about us, they cannot pull us down. But, on the other hand, if we are without the spirit of usefulness, if we are without morality, without liberality, without economy and property, without all those qualities which go to make a people and a nation great and strong, no matter what we may say about ourselves and what other people may say about us, we are losing ground. Nobody can give us those qualities merely by praising us and talking well about us; and when we possess them, nobody can take them from us by speaking ill of us.[1]

> What these men had in common was their love of God.

One cannot succeed with such genuine kindness toward others without embracing the presence of God's grace in their heart. The spirit of Tuskegee that Dr. Washington spoke of was real, winsome, and alive in the hearts of its leaders, faculty, and students. Dr. Washington embraced biblical standards for himself, and he stewarded Tuskegee Institute on the same standards.

In the Bible, King David was described as "a man after [God's] own heart" (1 Samuel 13:14). David was not satisfied to have his heart changed to be like God's; he pursued God's heart, as if to take it for his own. In essence, David was seeking a heart transplant. Booker T. Washington, George Washington Carver, and Robert Moton had kindred hearts and followed in the same pursuit. What these men had in common was their love for God and their fellow man and a heart to serve in making the world a better place.

George Washington Carver described how the "Tuskegee spirit" went out across the South, leaving its indelible mark:

> Washington's commencement addresses were unlike those of more orthodox schools, which stressed "success." Instead, he urged, "Go back to the place where you came from and work. Don't waste too much time looking for a paying job. If you can't get pay, ask for the privilege of working for nothing." In that spirit many left Tuskegee, the

nourishing mother of schools, and started offshoots
on the old plantations. You found a little Tuskegee
cropping up at a small settlement, at a crossroads,
in a shanty, an abandoned farm, a country store.
These educational outposts of an idea appeared in
South Carolina, Georgia, Mississippi, all the way
from Virginia to Texas. And they began to leaven
the economic life of the South.[2]

These words echo Dr. Washington's spirit to "cast down your
bucket where you are." It saddens me that we have allowed the
embers of the spirit of Tuskegee to grow cold and no longer retell
this beautiful and winsome story. We need this story, our kids
and grandkids need this story, to restore hope of unity among all
Americans. We owe it to the next generations to know that we
haven't always been as bad as we appear today. Our kids think
America is a bad place because they have little knowledge of how
far we have come. We've even forgotten where we came from, and
that's what needs repairing.

Professor Carver used the word *leaven*. The leaven of the
"Tuskegee spirit" is exactly what we need to soften our hearts
toward each other and celebrate what we have in common and
our victories in unity for the common good. My heart's desire is
for my kids and grandkids to learn from Dr. Washington, George
Washington Carver, and many other great men and women whose
stories are rich in the victim-to-victory narrative. Hopefully,
retelling Booker's story will begin the process of implementing the
narrative of his life into a culture that is starving for the relational
peace of Jesus.

Dr. Carver shared this story of how God revealed to him the
reason He made the peanut:

"Why did you make the peanut?" The Creator
said, "I have given you three laws; namely,

compatibility, temperature, and pressure. All you have to do is take these constituents and put them together, observing these laws, and 1 will show you why 1 made the peanut."[3]

Professor Carver worked his entire forty-seven-year career at Tuskegee Institute as the head of the Agriculture Department. During his tenure at Tuskegee, Professor Carver worked with two additional presidents. These men of the Black race would never have accomplished what they did without honoring God and living with a spirit of forgiveness. Booker T. Washington referred to this as the "Tuskegee spirit."

> *In farming, as in teaching, no matter where you go,*
> *remember to go with the "Tuskegee spirit."*
> —Booker T. Washington

Easy Like Sunday Morning

Lionel Richie is a product of Tuskegee. He accepted a tennis scholarship from Tuskegee University, graduating in 1974 with a bachelor's degree in economics, and attended graduate school at Auburn University.

His album *Easy Like Sunday Morning* was released in 1977, which was three years after 1 graduated from Harding University. The song "Easy (Like Sunday Morning)," written and sung by Lionel Richie, is one of my all-time favorites. While the lyrics have a powerful message, when you read between the lines, there is a deeper truth Lionel is interpreting. The song flows graciously, which makes it easy listening and easy to sing along to. 1 love the piano opening and the guitar solo. The line in the lyrics—"Girl, I'm leaving you tomorrow"—is perhaps what 1 most appreciate about the song. It speaks to whatever or whomever in our life is causing pain that we need freedom from. "Girl" could be a person, or the bondage of bitterness, anger, unforgiveness, or maybe even a job. Those words ring true for every single one of us in one way or another regarding the strongholds that keep us in emotional chains.

The word *easy* never brings a feeling of pressure or anxiety. Jesus said, "My yoke is easy and My burden is light" (Matthew 11:30). The question we must ask ourselves every day is, "Am I going to be easy today, or am I going to be difficult and hard to get along with?" This seems like a simple enough question, but it is truly one of the most difficult ways Jesus calls us to be like Him.

Someone said, "I love humanity; it's the people I can't stand." People make it hard to be easy, but that doesn't mean we have to match their bad attitude. When you get down to the bedrock, being "easy" is a choice we can make every day. It's something we have to do on purpose, so the next time you find yourself heating up in response to something or someone, take a breath, close your eyes, and play "Easy (Like Sunday Morning)." You will discover that singing along, low and slow with Lionel, will calm your spirit. We truly need to be easier to be around, easier to get along with, and easy about life, even when it ain't easy. Can I get an amen?

> *Love makes all things easy.*
> —Dwight L. Moody

Tuskegee Is Brotherhood

A brotherhood is a fellowship of people with common values, beliefs, and a family of integrated hearts that are in agreement in spirit. Ralph Ellison penned the following words about brotherhood in *Invisible Man*:

> *Brotherhood.* That's the word we got to keep right in front of our eyes every second. . . . We need a flag that stands for Brotherhood, and we need a sign we can wear . . . a pin or something like that. So that when a Brother meets a Brother they can know it.[4]

As I read Ellison's words, I realized we, too, need a sign, a way to identify each other as a Brother with a heart at rest in a weary world. *Tuskegee* is a Native American word meaning "warriors." Tuskegee is the perfect name for a Brotherhood of warriors for peace with hearts that say, "We are equal." Tuskegee will always be my personal symbol of peace and harmony, because it is neither Black nor White. Tuskegee is native and red, the color of our one Blood. We could wear "Tuskegee" on caps and T-shirts, as well as on bumper stickers, to declare the Brotherhood of equals, tender warriors who are of one heart, one blood, and one spirit. I have a couple of T-shirts I purchased at the campus bookstore at Tuskegee University. I love wearing those and displaying the Tuskegee name. I consider myself a Tuskegee American. A Tuskegee American has no ax to grind with anyone based on race or ethnicity. May "Tuskegee" become the symbol of kindness, mercy, and grace toward each other.

Imagine sitting in a restaurant or coffee shop and seeing someone across the room wearing the Tuskegee logo. Eye contact is made, followed by a smile and nod of affirmation, and both quietly mouth the word *Tuskegee*. Even if we do not speak the same language, the word *Tuskegee* speaks the peace and goodwill that is in our hearts. And how about wearing "Tuskegee" on the backs of football helmets? *Tuskegee* would become the all-in-one word for peace, goodwill, and equality among mankind.

The legacy of Booker T. Washington lives on today, and the excellence of Tuskegee is a reminder of who we could have become. Booker founded Tuskegee Normal and Industrial School on July 4, 1881. I will always celebrate our nation's independence on July 4th, but from now on I will also celebrate Booker T. Washington and Tuskegee as the most excellent institute of higher education the world has ever witnessed. We could even declare the Sunday following July 4th as Tuskegee Celebration Day. Together, we could worship, break bread, listen, pray, celebrate holy communion, and integrate our hearts together as members of the Tuskegee Brotherhood of all nations in celebration of the goodness of God.

God manifested His love, grace, and mercy on the grounds of

Tuskegee at a time when His enemy was lurking to steal, kill, and destroy what was in the hearts of Booker T. Washington, George Washington Carver, and the tender warriors of Tuskegee. We will never agree on everything, but we can be united again, like Booker Washington said: "As separate as the fingers, yet one as the hand."[5]

The Tuskegee movement could become just what the good old USA needs to close the gap that divides us. Let's make Dr. Washington's vision and Dr. King's dream come true in the spirit of Tuskegee. Please join me and let's become Tuskegee Americans together.

TUSKEGEE!
Together we Unite in Spirit and Kindness Essential for Grace Eternally Equal

I love you is forever. The only words that the world wants to hear. We're a family and not a tribe. We're a family and not a party. We're a family. The day that happens we will clearly be united together as one.
—Lionel Richie

CHAPTER FOURTEEN

It's Time for Grace

The most important thing in your life is not what you do;
it's who you become. That's what you will take into eternity.
—Dallas Willard

Living the Dream

Frederick Douglass, Booker T. Washington, and Dr. Martin Luther King all dreamed of a day when Blacks and Whites would show the world what peace on earth looks like. While that dream is closer to becoming a reality, we still have a long way to go because of the continued distortion of what is true. We are led to believe that if you are White, you are evil, and if you are Black, you are a victim with no hope. Both are lies from the pit of hell. The truth is, every one of us is evil by nature, but because of the love of God and the finished work of Jesus, we live out of His goodness. This is the truth, whether you believer it or not. Jesus is our hope—hope for now and hope for what is to come.

Booker T. Washington came to Tuskegee as a result of two men with an idea, a seed planted by God—one Black and one White, working together for the purpose of raising up the man farthest down. Booker accomplished what he did because his plan and methods for education and personal development were grounded in bedrock biblical values. They worked and made perfect sense to the many high-character White men and women who became partners with Booker, Professor Carver, and those who made Tuskegee Institute the beacon of light that continues to shine in a dark and depraved world.

Men of all colors and walks of life have historically joined forces for a common good. In every war America has deployed men and women of every nationality, fighting side by side for the purpose of defending freedom from evil's advance, though not always getting it right. We remain at war today, but it is a war of a different kind. The war raging today begins with our thoughts and how we allow those thoughts to become words or actions of impulse. How we steward our thoughts ultimately determines whether our actions are a blessing or a condemnation. One thing that helps us steward our thoughts is that we must stop making assumptions that are simply not true. Booker T. Washington showed us how to live and do business out of selflessness, with noble character, integrity, and peace of mind. Is this not what we all desire? Are we so driven by our own self that we have lost all ability to humble ourselves and surrender our will for the will of God? If you truly desire to live in a calmer environment, I encourage you to begin living the life lessons of Booker T. Washington and then sharing them with those you love. Booker pointed us to the true source of peace through his knowledge, wisdom, and character by the way he lived and loved. Booker pointed us to Jesus.

In his book *Teddy and Booker T.*, Brian Kilmeade gave an account of what we can accomplish when we work together for a common purpose. He described the scene as Teddy Roosevelt led his band of Rough Riders up San Juan Hill on the island of Cuba in the summer of 1898. Describing Roosevelt, Kilmeade wrote, "He had put himself at the center of an extraordinary venture. With him at the head, an army of Harvard men and Confederate generals, cowboys and Native Americans, Yankee and Southerners, Black men and White men, ballplayers and gentlemen had fought side by side."[1]

You and I are "at the center of an extraordinary venture" in America today. What goes on in our mind is determined by who is in authority of our life. The same is true in America. We are a mosaic of nations and ethnicities, with varying colors of skin, all created to glorify our Creator God, yet His enemy uses our differences to effectively divide us and steal our joy in the process. This does not have to be the case, even though the voices of evil people continue to distort the truth. God created us for the purpose of fellowship with Him, and because of His grace, He gives us everything we need to be at peace with Him, peace with ourselves, and peace with each other. He gives us a person we can relate to, and His name is Jesus.

The classic movie *The Shawshank Redemption* is a story of two inmates who were destined to become friends. Morgan Freeman played the part of Red, a Black man, and Tim Robbins played Andy, a White banker, both convicted of murder. They became good friends, and in the last scene in the movie, Red recalls something Andy said one day in the prison yard. Andy said, "Remember, Red, hope is a good thing, maybe the best of things, and no good thing ever dies."[2]

The redemptive stories of hope are the ones that help us remember who we are, where we came from, and where we are going. Whether our ancestors came from Europe, India, Asia, or by force from Africa, we are all together now. We are a family, and because our ultimate Hope is in Jesus, we can live with hope of peace on earth. It is time our people, all of our people, learn the truth that there was goodness in our past and remember those men and women of noble character who have lasting influence on the hearts of the people and the soul of our nation. Whether Jew or Greek, slave or free, male or female, we are one in the eyes of God. Bottom line, we have a choice, and it boils down to who has the final word in our life. We all live under the authority of someone or something. Coming to grips with the reality of who that authority is determines whether we live the abundant life of grace, at peace with our fellowman. Whether we believe it or not, God will have the final word. The choice you and I make is critical to who we are personally, but also in how we influence those in our circle. The choice we make determines whether we live to bless or to condemn. As you and I go, so goes the country. Let's choose Jesus together as "blessers" of the critical grace of God.

Brennan Manning is still right: "All is grace."[3]

> *Unless there is within us that which is above us,*
> *we shall soon yield to that which is about us.*
> *The first duty of every soul is to find not its*
> *freedom but its master.*
> —P. T. Forsyth

Afterword

By Dudley Hall

Even though God has assured us that He still owns all things and that He has done all that is necessary to restore all things to His design, we find ourselves more focused on the obvious evil and injustice in our world than on the evidences of grace that abound. Looking back, in the midst of willful blindness on the part of the church and American society, as slavery and later racial prejudice were tolerated, God was not silent or passive. He was raising up those whom society ignored to show His mercy and exalt His strength. It is consistent with His ways.

> Has not God made foolish the wisdom of the world? . . . Not many of you were wise by human standards; not many were influential; not many were of noble birth. But God chose the foolish things of the world to shame the wise; God chose the weak things of the world to shame the strong. (1 Corinthians 1:20, 26-27, NIV)

What He was doing in Tuskegee, Alabama, with Booker T. Washington and his cohorts was monumental. It was overlooked at the time, but the seeds of the kingdom of God were being planted, and those seeds would inevitably sprout and bring forth the fruit of that kingdom. They can't be ignored now. We can see that right in the heart of Dixie, God planted a seed in the heart of a man who has consistently given light to darkness and pushed back the onslaught of hell's intention to divide and devalue God's creation. The march still proceeds; the fight still goes on. But the God who started it will see to it that His work never fails. We are first embarrassed that our own land could be so selfishly blind, and then we are encouraged that there was always a light in the darkness. God always has a Booker T. Washington that He is willing to raise up when He desires. We are thankful. We are also challenged to stop and look around. What are we blind to now? Who is God raising up to shine to the light? Might it be me?

How far you go in life depends on your being tender with the young,
compassionate with the aged, sympathetic with the striving
and tolerant of the weak and strong. Because someday in your life
you will have been all of these.
—George Washington Carver

Think about it: we went into slavery pagans; we came out Christians.
We went into slavery pieces of property; we came out American citizens.
We went into slavery with chains clanking about our wrists;
we came out with the American ballot in our hands.
—Booker T. Washington

About the Author

Cecil Carder was in the hunting and fishing industry for thirty-five years. Spring turkey hunting and chasing elk in September are among his greatest passions. While he loves fishing of all types, he favors catching small-mouth bass and floating a fly in a mountain stream. Cecil and Dianne have been married for fifty-two years; they have two children and six grandchildren. Cecil loves to hear a good story, especially when told by a gifted storyteller. He believes the art of storytelling has been lost but can be rediscovered when we include God, who is in our stories whether we acknowledge Him or not. Cecil is also the author of *Narrowtive* which was published in 2021. Cecil and Dianne reside in Fort Worth, Texas, where he continues to write and serve in the kingdom. He and Dianne enjoy being Texans again.

Endnotes

Introduction

1. Ralph Ellison, *Invisible Man* (New York: Random House, 1952).
2. Stephen Mansfield, *Men on Fire* (Grand Rapids, MI: Baker Books, 2020), 23.
3. Edith Powell, *More Than Peanuts: The Unlikely Partnership of Tom Huston and George Washington Carver* (Athens, GA: NewSouth Books, 2022).
4. Booker T. Washington, *Up from Slavery* (Garden City, NY: Doubleday & Company, 1901), https://docsouth.unc.edu/fpn/washington/washing.html.
5. Lawrence W. Reed, "Why Booker T. Washington Remains a Model for the Ages," FEE Stories, February 26, 2023, https://fee.org/articles/why-booker-t-washington-remains-a-model-for-the-ages/.
6. Martin Luther King Jr., "I Have a Dream," delivered August 28, 1963, at the Lincoln Memorial, Washington, DC, https://www.americanrhetoric.com/speeches/mlkihaveadream.htm.
7. Washington, *Up from Slavery*.
8. Nicholas Ballasy, "Denzel Washington on Race Relations: 'You Can't Legislate Love,'" PJMedia, December 7, 2016, https://pjmedia.com/nicholas-ballasy/2016/12/07/denzel-washington-on-race-relations-you-cant-legislate-love-n105641.
9. Brennan Manning, *All Is Grace* (Colorado Springs, CO: David C Cook, 2011).

Chapter 1

1. Booker T. Washington, ed., *Tuskegee and Its People*, Booker T. Washington, "General Introduction" (New York: D. Appleton and Company, 1906), https://www.gutenberg.org/files/28087/28087-h/28087-h.htm#i20.
2. Booker T. Washington, *Up from Slavery* (Garden City, NY: Doubleday & Company, 1901), https://docsouth.unc.edu/fpn/washington/washing.html.

3. James E. Ward Jr., *Zero Victim: Overcoming Injustice with a New Attitude* (Warrenton, VA: Freiling Publishing, 2021).

4. Ward, *Zero Victim*.

5. Nelson Mandela, *Long Walk to Freedom* (Boston: Little, Brown and Company, 1995).

Chapter 2

1. Robert R. Moton, "A Life of Achievement," February 11, 1916, https://www.blackpast.org/african-american-history/1916-robert-r-moton-life-achievement/.

2. Washington, *Up from Slavery*.

3. Washington, *Up from Slavery*.

4. Washington, *Up from Slavery*.

5. Washington, *Up from Slavery*.

6. Booker T. Washington, *My Larger Education* (Garden City, NY: Doubleday, Page and Company, 1911), https://docsouth.unc.edu/fpn/washeducation/washing.html#:~:text=lt%20was%20only%20gradually%20that,own%20race%20would%20be%20of.

7. Washington, *Up from Slavery*.

8. Washington, *Up from Slavery*.

9. Washington, *Up from Slavery*.

10. John Piper, "God Is Most Glorified in Us When We Are Most Satisfied in Him," October 13, 2012, https://www.desiringgod.org/messages/god-is-most-glorified-in-us-when-we-are-most-satisfied-in-him.

11. "Booker T. Washington Delivers the 1895 Atlanta Compromise Speech," https://courses.lumenlearning.com/suny-tc3-ushistory1os/chapter/primary-source-atlanta-compromise-speech-1895/.

12. Henri J. M. Nouwen, *The Inner Voice of Love* (New York: Image Books, 1998), 31.

13. *Elf*, directed by Jon Favreau, 2003.

14. Washington, *My Larger Education*.

15. Washington, *My Larger Education*.

Chapter 3

1. Booker T. Washington, *Up from Slavery* (Garden City, NY: Doubleday & Company, 1901), https://docsouth.unc.edu/fpn/washington/washing.html.

2. Washington, *Up from Slavery*.
3. Washington, *Up from Slavery*.
4. Washington, *Up from Slavery*.
5. Washington, *Up from Slavery*.
6. Washington, *My Larger Education*.

Chapter 4

1. Booker T. Washington, *My Larger Education* (Garden City, NY: Doubleday, Page and Company, 1911), https://docsouth.unc.edu/fpn/washeducation/washing.html#:~:text=lt%20was%20only%20gradually%20that,own%20race%20would%20be%20of.
2. Washington, *My Larger Education*.
3. Washington, *My Larger Education*.
4. Washington, *My Larger Education*.
5. Washington, *My Larger Education*.
6. Washington, *My Larger Education*.
7. Booker T. Washington, *Up from Slavery* (Garden City, NY: Doubleday & Company, 1901), https://docsouth.unc.edu/fpn/washington/washing.html.
8. Washington, *Up from Slavery*.

Chapter 5

1. Brennan Manning, *All Is Grace* (Colorado Springs, CO: David C Cook, 2011).
2. Booker T. Washington, *Up from Slavery* (Garden City, NY: Doubleday & Company, 1901), https://docsouth.unc.edu/fpn/washington/washing.html.
3. Washington, *Up from Slavery*.
4. Booker T. Washington, *Character Building* (New York: Doubleday, Page and Company, 1902), https://www.gutenberg.org/cache/epub/60484/pg60484-images.html.
5. Booker T. Washington, *My Larger Education* (Garden City, NY: Doubleday, Page and Company, 1911), https://docsouth.unc.edu/fpn/washeducation/washing.html#:~:text=lt%20was%20only%20gradually%20that,own%20race%20would%20be%20of.

Chapter 6

1. Booker T. Washington, *Character Building* (New York: Doubleday, Page and Company, 1902), https://www.gutenberg.org/cache/epub/60484/pg60484-images.html.
2. Kathy Koch, PhD, *Parent Differently: Raise Kids with Biblical Character That Changes Culture* (Chicago: Moody Publishers, 2023).
3. Washington, *Character Building*.
4. Washington, *Character Building*.
5. Washington, *Character Building*.
6. Washington, *Character Building*.
7. Washington, *Character Building*.
8. Washington, *Character Building*.
9. Washington, *Character Building*.
10. Washington, *Character Building*.
11. Booker T. Washington, ed., *Tuskegee and Its People*, Booker T. Washington, "Preface" (New York: D. Appleton and Company, 1906), https://www.gutenberg.org/files/28087/28087-h/28087-h.htm#i20.
12. Washington, ed., *Tuskegee and Its People*, Booker T. Washington, "General Introduction."

Chapter 7

1. Carter G. Woodson, PhD, ed., *Negro Orators and Their Orations*, Robert R. Moton, "A Life of Achievement" (Washington, DC: The Associated Publishers, 1925), 604, https://www.google.com/books/edition/Negro_Orators_and_Their_Orations/SsNlAAAAMAAJ?hl=&gbpv=1.

Chapter 8

1. Carol M. Swain and Christopher J. Schorr, *Black Eye for America* (Be the People Books, 2021).
2. Booker T. Washington, *My Larger Education* (Garden City, NY: Doubleday, Page and Company, 1911), https://docsouth.unc.edu/fpn/washeducation/washing.html#:~:text=It%20was%20only%20gradually%20that,own%20race%20would%20be%20of.
3. C. Herbert Woolston, "Jesus Loves the Little Children," 1864.
4. Voddie Baucham, "Fault Lines Study: Introduction," YouTube, https://www.youtube.com/watch?v=7m8E_9Q5WGI.

5. David Hookstead, "Michigan OC Sherrone Moore Faces Heat for Saying He Doesn't See Race," OutKick, December 30, 2023, https://www.outkick.com/sherrone-moore-doesnt-see-race-criticism-reaction/.

6. Daniel Patrick Moynihan, "The Moynihan Report: The Negro Family, The Case for National Action," March 1965, https://www.blackpast.org/african-american-history/moynihan-report-1965/.

7. Moynihan, "The Moynihan Report: The Negro Family, The Case for National Action," https://www.blackpast.org/african-american-history/moynihan-report-1965/.

Chapter 9

1. David Holland, *Praying Grace for Men* (Seattle: BroadStreet Publishing Group, 2022).

2. Emma Lazarus, "The New Colossus," 1883, https://www.poetryfoundation.org/poems/46550/the-new-colossus.

3. Booker T. Washington, *Up from Slavery* (Garden City, NY: Doubleday & Company, 1901), https://docsouth.unc.edu/fpn/washington/washing.html.

4. Booker T. Washington, *Character Building* (New York: Doubleday, Page and Company, 1902), https://www.gutenberg.org/cache/epub/60484/pg60484-images.html.

5. Washington, *Up from Slavery*.

6. Booker T. Washington, ed., *Tuskegee and Its People*, Emmet J. Scott, "Present Achievements and Governing Ideals" (New York: D. Appleton and Company, 1906), https://www.gutenberg.org/files/28087/28087-h/28087-h.htm#i20.

7. Washington, *Up from Slavery*.

8. Washington, *Character Building*.

Chapter 10

1. Brant Hansen, *Unoffendable* (Nashville: W Publishing, 2015).

2. Booker T. Washington, Goodreads.com, https://www.goodreads.com/quotes/168477-egotism-is-the-anesthetic-that-dulls-the-pain-of-stupidity.

3. Shelby Steele, *White Guilt: How Blacks and Whites Together Destroyed the Promise of the Civil Rights Era* (New York: HarperCollins, 2006).

4. Lyndon B. Johnson, "Commencement Address at Howard University: 'To Fulfill These Rights," June 4, 1965, https://www.presidency.ucsb.edu/documents/commencement-address-howard-university-fulfill-these-rights.

5. "Uncommon Knowledge with Hoover Fellow Shelby Steele and the Weekly Standard's Bill Kristol," October 16, 2012, https://www.youtube.com/watch?v=DNRkWLlKDoI.

6. Paul David Tripp, *New Morning Mercies: A Daily Gospel Devotional*, "January 25"(Wheaton, IL: Crossway, 2014).

Chapter 11

1. Ralph Ellison, *Invisible Man* (New York: Random House, 1952).

2. Paul David Tripp, *New Morning Mercies* (Wheaton, IL: Crossway, 2014).

3. Brian Kilmeade, *Teddy and Booker T.: How Two American Icons Blazed a Path for Racial Equality* (New York: Sentinel, 2023), 271.

4. Booker T. Washington, *Up from Slavery* (Garden City, NY: Doubleday & Company, 1901), https://docsouth.unc.edu/fpn/washington/washing.html.

Chapter 12

1. Booker T. Washington, *Up from Slavery* (Garden City, NY: Doubleday & Company, 1901), https://docsouth.unc.edu/fpn/washington/washing.html.

2. Louis R. Harlan, ed., *The Booker T. Washington Papers* (Champaign, IL: University of Illinois Press, 1981).

3. David Takle, *The Truth About Lies and Lies About Truth* (High Point, NC: Kingdom Formation Ministries, 2017).

4. Lionel Richie, AZquotes, https://www.azquotes.com/quote/1427857.

5. Read the full story in Genesis 3.

Chapter 13

1. Booker T. Washington, *Character Building* (New York: Doubleday, Page and Company, 1902), https://www.gutenberg.org/cache/epub/60484/pg60484-images.html.

2. Rackham Holt, *George Washington Carver* (Garden City, NY: Doubleday & Company, Inc, 1963).

3. Edith Powell, *More Than Peanuts: The Unlikely Partnership of Tom Huston and George Washington Carver* (Athens, GA: NewSouth Books, 2022).

4. Ralph Ellison, *Invisible Man* (New York: Random House, 1952), 394–395.

5. Booker T. Washington, *Up from Slavery* (Garden City, NY: Doubleday & Company, 1901), https://docsouth.unc.edu/fpn/washington/washing.html.

Chapter 14

1. Brian Kilmeade, *Teddy and Booker T.: How Two American Icons Blazed a Path for Racial Equality* (New York: Sentinel, 2023).

2. *The Shawshank Redemption*, directed by Frank Darabont, 1994.

3. Brennan Manning, *All Is Grace* (Colorado Springs, CO: David C Cook, 2011).

To purchase additional copies of this book,
please visit kerygmaventures.com

Printed in the USA
CPSIA information can be obtained
at www.ICGtesting.com
LVHW020412040524
779077LV00002B/4